For You

Andreas Seidl

Handover of Power

European Version

Volume 2: Derivation

Imprint

Bibliographic information of the German National Library:
The German National Library lists this publication in the
German National Bibliography; detailed bibliographic data
are available on the Internet at http://dnb.dnb.de.

© 2022 Dipl. Pol. Theodor Andreas Seidl

Cover: Christiane Ebrecht
Translation: DeepL, Cologne
Production and publishing: BoD – Books on Demand,
Norderstedt

ISBN: 978-3-7568-0235-7

Acknowledgements

My thanks go to my family and friends who have made me who I am today. Special thanks to all those who supported me in writing this book. I would like to thank all my classmates, teachers, fellow students, lecturers, demonstrators, activists, colleagues, companies and countries with whom I have had the privilege of sharing the experiences from which all the ideas in this book have emerged. I would like to thank the staff of Books on Demand for their kind helpfulness. I thank the citizens of Seligenstadt for the harmony and solidarity in which I was able to write.

Foreword

This policy concept contains a variety of proposals for possible political reforms. It can be peacefully and democratically adapted to any current political system of any state in the world, but also to political systems in families, clubs, associations or companies. Wherever humans make or submit to rules that manage living together, the following proposals can be helpful. Readers who find the proposals so helpful that they would like to implement them together with like-minded people can contact the author. The contact form on the last page can be used for this purpose.

Faults and defects
I ask for your understanding that this volume was not professionally proofread. I could only afford professional proofreading for the summary. Spelling errors and unfortunate phrasing may therefore occur. As soon as this volume has sold enough to pay for a professional proofreading, it will be done. After that, a new edition will be published.

English version
Please understand that this volume has been translated automatically. I could only afford a professional translation for the summary. Poor wording and spelling errors may therefore occur. In case of doubt, the German version shall prevail. As soon as this volume has sold enough to pay for a professional translation, it will be done. After that, a new edition will be

published. It was more important to me that no one in the world should have an information advantage than individual translation errors in the complete work.

Table of contents

1 Introduction

I became interested in politics when I was about 17. In the beginning, I stood with school friends and we grumbled about politics. That's when I realised that it made me unhappy just to complain and not be able to do anything about it. So I wanted to think of solutions and talk about them rather than problems. I started to write down all my ideas in a diary. My intention was to turn them into a party programme that could be used to found a party. My hope was to be able to make a difference. My fear was that I would end up as an old man who only grumbles and is angry that he never tried to solve the problems.

This is how my mission for the handover of power began. In the beginning, the goal was "You must know your enemies in order to be able to fight them", later it became "You must become the head of government in order to effectively solve the problems" and today it is "Change the current system and thus save humanity". These ever-increasing goals became necessary because I realised that further down in the system I could not eliminate the cause, but only mitigate the effect. Colloquially, one says: "The fish stinks from the head." So it was clear where I had to start. I also noticed that many humans were affected, worldwide.

I wanted to know who was responsible for this and get to know this person. It was not until the last final exam of my political science degree and after numerous internships in the halls of power that I found the answer. It is not a single human or a group of humans. It is a flawed system to which humans have adapted. I was able to identify four faults that are so central that they are the cause of all the problems that follow. The faults cause human behaviour that does more damage than good to humanity. The good thing about this is firstly the realisation that no human is inherently evil or stupid. Only in living together with other humans do they adapt to a system made by humans. The good thing is that we humans created this system, so we can change it. All we need is a procedure that not only allows us to adapt, but also gives us the opportunity to question the adaptation and, if necessary, to recognise and correct faults.

2 Summary

This volume serves to present the need for the other volumes through problems, solutions and examples, as well as the intention of this book. First, I will name the faults in the system and the resulting problems and underline them with examples. This is followed by approaches to solutions, which are described in detail in all volumes of the book. At the end, I will give an insight into my personality and which basic attitudes have influenced me in writing this book. Finally, I turn to you personally, dear reader. I give you hints to help you read and understand and how you can join in if you feel like doing so after reading the book.

3 Purpose of the book

The purpose of the book is to give all humans in the world a proposal on how they can peacefully take power in their state. After the democratic handover of power, they can democratically shape their lives together in a self-determined way. From the very beginning, this book was to become a party programme so that humans all over the world could found this party and run for election. Known party programmes, however, usually remain very vague in their statements about reforms and proposed solutions. Election programmes and government programmes are more precise. However, this gives voters incomplete information about the vision that a party is pursuing.

The name of the new party is Dynamic People's Party. It is dynamic because citizens can have more or less say, depending on their willingness to participate. Citizens can also live close to nature or technically, with a lot or little free time, money, like-minded people or neighbours, depending on their attitudes to life. They can change their attitudes several times in their lives, whenever it suits them. Most of the time, this is left up to them if no one else is affected. Often, a minimum number of humans is needed if a group of affected people wants to create its own rules in a delimited area. This is So-called minority protection. The majority determines the generally applicable rules in the form of the constitution, the laws and the election of politicians. This is where the name People's Party comes from, because every single citizen in the people and every policy area is included and it is not an issue party.

3.1 Division of the 21 volumes

With its 21 volumes, the book contains all the necessary information for the handover of power. In the volume summarising all the other 20 volumes, humans can quickly get an overview and create a party programme. In the derivation volume, readers are told what problems in the policy system and views of the author led to the proposals in the other volumes. The derivation can be used in election campaigns. The 18 volumes on the ministries and the volume on the constitution form the government programme. The derivation and the government programme can be used to prepare election programmes for individual elections involving different areas of accountability. The adaptations are made possible by using only the appropriate chapters from each volume. These contents then only need to be adapted to the respective current and local circumstances. Families, clubs, companies, cities, municipalities, regions, countries, confederations and international organisations can use the political contents, processes and structures to deal with each other more peacefully and effectively.

3.2 Target group of the book

All humans of the earth are part of the target group of this book, because they belong to the humanity that this book wants to save. The book is written in an understandable language with as few foreign words as possible, which are described when they first appear. There is no group of humans that is oppressed. Everyone can be the architect of his or her own fortune without causing damage to others. All humans worldwide have the same needs. Each individual wants to give and receive sufficient air, water, food, health, clothing, living space, affection, as well as separation and commonality from and with other humans. The natural need of our species is for humanity to survive. This book provides proposals on how all these needs can be met for all humans and humanity. Even if there are humans who do not like proposals, the book contains ways in which these humans can create their own proposals and put them to the citizens or party members for election. This makes it possible to involve any opposition in order to win over an absolute majority of voters for the party programme as quickly as possible. The divide between right and left will be eliminated because the policy areas will offer suitable solutions for right and left voters.

3.3 Risks in the handover of power

A change of power in the form of a peaceful revolution carries the risk of chaos after the disempowerment, because it is not clear how power will be redistributed and to whom. That is why this book is so extensive. If a majority is to be mobilised to change the current system with its rulers, then it must be clear to everyone what will happen before, during and after the handover of power. This takes away the fear of all participants as to what their future will look like and that they would have to fear for their lives afterwards. Economic relations in particular thus receive legal certainty. Private and state relations receive planning security. In order to make the handover of power as smooth and non-violent as possible, new rules are gradually introduced and old rules are dismantled. The participants set the pace by asking for their opinions through surveys and voting. Politicians who do not adhere to the programmes determined in their election of persons are replaced.

The book offers a novel form of governance that can be adapted to all current political systems in the world. This means private, economic and state systems, but the book focuses on state political management. This new kind of political system works as fast, digitally, democratically and profit-oriented as no political system before. This eliminates the risk of states not changing rapidly after the handover of power. The new form of government is a reinsurance for voters and against dictators.

Top candidates and party leaders of the new dynamic People's Party become heads of government or presidents of a state if they win the elections, but they abolish this office in their first term with an absolute majority. They then distribute power among 18 ministers and directly elected politicians for specific offices. Decision-makers become electable and as soon as a majority of voters is found, new elections are held. The book can also be abused if the participants, minorities or the people are not affected. Then only certain proposals would be implemented without introducing the new form of government. For this case, there is the chapter on State Security in the Ministry of State Organisation. It says how the people can take back power from autocrats or electoral fraudsters.

The book offers a chapter on the changeover to the new system for each ministry. This makes it clear which measures will be necessary after the handover of power in each individual policy area. There is a risk here of not having taken into account all the circumstances that apply to the respective system. In this book, the changeover is illustrated using the example of Germany. In the case of a family, city, municipality, organisation, club, company, confederation or other country, appropriate requirements must be made without which the changeover cannot be completed.

3.4 Aims of the book

This book comes from the author's diary of ideas when he was rethinking policy. While studying theory and practice, he saw himself as a social researcher and system designer. Over two decades, this resulted in a new world order called "dynamic media democracy". The name describes a policy system of how humanity can be unleashed to form a new world in which it wants to live. Individual humans communicate via the media and thus become active together as humanity. External determination by individuals is abolished. Politically unstable conditions are peacefully transformed into long-term stable and innovative conditions. Using four economic forms, individuals can decide for more or less freedom or security and join forces with like-minded people. The new worldview can be implemented by small communities, but also by all states in the world. The scope of application is scalable and thus dissemination can proceed quickly and across the board. The book contains proposals for the democratisation of one place and the whole world, world peace, the united states of the world and the future of humanity. It describes the beginning of a new attitude towards life, the end of disenchantment with politics and a democracy in which the common good can flourish. Except in the derivation, nothing and no one is criticised, only solutions are offered without describing the associated problems. Through the proposed solutions, the people learn a way to empower themselves. Whether these descriptions remain fiction or become reality is for each reader to decide. Each volume contains a contact form on the last page to get involved.

Metaphorically speaking, humanity is embarking on a journey to a new world. It knows where the journey is going, what paths and obstacles there are and sets off unstoppably full of drive. It makes faults along the way, learns from them and celebrates its small and large successes.

The political concept of this book can be adapted to any current system of any state in the world. Using Germany as an example, the handover of power is made clear through the formation of a party, participation in elections to parliament, the formation of a government and the government programme for all ministries. Participation in elections can be possible in different ways in different countries. The decisive factor is the election from which a government emerges. Depending on whether the election is for the government of a city, a region, a federal state or an entire country, only the applicable parts are taken from the volumes of this book. Exactly which parts are extracted depends on the areas of accountability that the government in question has and that are related to the corresponding department.

Undemocratic states that do not elect their government democratically are in the mode of indirect democracy, where ministers decide and act on their own authority, but without opportunities for citizens to participate. Citizens must first obtain these opportunities for co-determination. How they can do this peacefully and democratically is described in the volumes on state organisation and derivation. In this volume, the chapter on a power vacuum in revolutions describes the procedure that becomes necessary after a revolution.

For assistance, there is a contact form on the last page. Readers can send it to be linked by the author through the contact details provided. They can then form a party for implementation or join a party that wants to implement this new policy concept.

Current rulers of democratic or undemocratic states can also initiate the handover of power to the people themselves by gradually switching to the new system. To do this, they can first create the necessary conditions and then have the deputy ministers elected in all municipalities. Presumably, their people will thank them for this step by electing them in a direct election and only deselecting them as soon as they persistently violate the will of the people. What is decisive is that this new policy system will make more prosperity possible worldwide because it will function more economically and innovatively.

4 Problems, solutions, examples

In the following chapter, I list the crucial problems that led me to develop the ideas for suitable solutions. In this way, I would like to create the possibility of being able to understand my thought processes. The problems and solutions are described in chapters with the same names as the volumes of the ministries affected. The sub-chapters are appropriate names for the faults in the current system. I have either thought up examples, described them in detail in other volumes or experienced them myself.

4.1 State organisation

Three of the four central faults can be found in the political system of organising states. Therefore, it became necessary to invent a new political system. The current system protects itself with its mass. By having so many laws and treaties that cover hundreds of pages, it becomes impossible for an individual to understand the system. In the complexity, individual connections of meaning get lost. However, they are still effective, even if no human can oversee them. That is why a policy system should be based on concise, easy-to-understand rules.

4.1.1 Interdepartmental parties

The first central fault lies in the party system. Each party covers all policy remits. Voters can only vote for or be a member of one party, even though they like different proposals for different remits from several parties. They have no choice but to vote for the least evil. For example, it is not possible to support the environmental policy of the Greens, the labour market policy of the Socialists, the defence policy of the Left, the financial policy of the Conservatives, the data protection policy of the Pirates, the education policy of the Liberals and the immigration policy of the Right. In the end, this state of affairs leads to voters making their decisions not on the basis of content, but with emotion and sympathy. Manipulating these emotions is easier than convincing them with better arguments. Election advertising therefore likes to play on hope and fear. This has an effect on humans in that they do not learn to give preference to the better argument. They influence the feelings of the other person by acting or simply imitating the behaviour of a role model.

A solution in the current system would only be possible if voters knew all the election and party programmes, categorised them uniformly according to remits and knew which politician was responsible for what and in which European, national, regional, local or municipal election that politician would be decided. This excessive demand gives the voter the feeling of being a helpless victim, a pawn in a policy that he or she does not understand. In this case of disorientation, the human being blindly follows the leader of the herd, or he turns away from the herd in disgruntlement, or he rebels aimlessly against the system without knowing exactly why. Editors and reporters in the press are also affected by this excessive demand and therefore prefer to report emotionally and refer to persons instead of programmes and facts.

When I joined political parties myself, I learned that all parties have working groups for different policy remits. There, approaches to solutions are developed and opinions on current government policy are found. So I thought these working groups could become the party wings of their remit in the new system and give it the name of their party. For example, the working group responsible for labour policy in an existing party in the country can create the party wing in the Labour Party with the same name.

The solution is one party per remit with any number of party wings. The 18 remits are Labour, Foreign Affairs, Education, Digital, Family, Finance, Health, Infrastructure, Innovation, Integration, Justice, Media, Security, State Organisation, Barter Economy, Planned Economy, Social Market Economy, Free Market Economy. Only one party is responsible for each remit. In elections, only one remit is up for debate. For example, the education party could have a party wing that is for frontal teaching and a party wing for project teaching.

In this way, humans learn to think for themselves and to take responsibility for their own deciders. They then act more responsibly and with more foresight. As a mass of people in a democratically organised system, they can develop a swarm intelligence that ensures the survival of humanity.

4.1.2 Irresponsible politicians

The second central fault lies in the electoral system. Voters cannot hold individual politicians responsible and deselect them in case of failure. Chains of legitimacy are created when voters elect a parliamentarian, who elects a government president, who appoints ministers. If the voter does not like the behaviour of a minister, he cannot specifically deselect him. If that minister then makes laws, all parliamentarians decide to do so. The voter no longer has the possibility to change individual laws. When he votes, he would have to know all the decisions of all the ministers and parliamentarians in order to make his decision. Since he has to do this for all political levels over a period of years, this flood of information overwhelms him. In the domestic electorate, for example, voters have to consider the following political levels: the European, national, regional, local or municipal parliament, as well as the mayor. Only in the case of the mayor is there no chain of legitimacy, because he is directly connected to the voter.

For the voter, this means an opaque network of responsibilities across all remits and political levels. This forces them to think in general terms and to rate only the overall situation without knowing who is responsible for their satisfaction or dissatisfaction. Humans thus learn to reject or approve of things, conditions or people across the board without having to know the reason. He increasingly accepts arguments from like-minded people and rejects other arguments without questioning them. This enables manipulation through opposing opinions that divide the population. The divided population is set against each other in order to be able to shift responsibility to the respective opposing side in the population instead of to responsible politicians. The feeling of insecurity triggers fear in the human. Fear in turn sets the fear-hate circuit in the brain in motion. An action that triggers fear is met with a reaction of hatred against oneself or others, which in turn generates fear. As soon as the fear trigger is not clearly identifiable, hatred is discharged against some fashionable enemy image. For example, increased drug use is a reaction to fear with an invisible originator. In this case, hatred is discharged against oneself through damage to one's own body. Hatred against immigrants through bodily harm or damage to property is an example of a politically generated enemy image. It is striking that humans choose drugs with which to damage themselves. Enemy images, on the other hand, are first created by a certain policy. For example, immigration policy is responsible for immigration in the country and not the immigrant himself.

As a party member of various parties, I learned how politicians get into office. Whoever has the best rope of party members in decisive positions gets to the top of their party's electoral list. Ideas, content, skills, knowledge or experience hardly play a role and are certainly no guarantee for a place on the list. Ideas or content tend to come from the working groups or are offered to the candidates at the top of the list. This gave me the colloquial impression that "to get to the top you have to crawl through a thousand asses and in the end you're no longer who you were at the beginning." So I decided to design a new election procedure that would allow the direct election of the deciding persons in ministries.

The solution is the direct election of politicians. Politicians are all ministers, their deputies from each municipality, as well as responsible persons in an agency, such as a judge or the head of the Central Bank. The election procedure is split. First, the programme is decided in a pre-election and then, in the run-off election, the candidate who is to execute it. For example, in the pre-election for education minister, frontal teaching and project teaching are in two different programmes. Project teaching wins and the candidate with experience in project teaching wins the run-off election. This is followed by his induction period and in-service studies if he does not yet have the necessary expertise for his office.

4.1.3 Short-term decisions with long-term damage

The third central fault lies in the fixed electoral periods. Election periods are always short-term, usually 4 to 6 years. A people, however, consists of generations of humans who pursue medium- and long-term goals in their lives and are aware of these goals. Politicians, in the meantime, can no longer be punished by voters if they break election promises or react wrongly to unforeseen incidents. Voters would have to keep records themselves of which politicians of which parties have made serious faults for them, which they can punish in the coming election. In the coming election, however, the party of the wrongdoers may then draw up a good programme for the coming election period. Voters have to decide whether they would rather punish politicians for their past deeds or have a say in the future.

Politicians tend to make short-term decisions at the expense of the long term, because they are no longer responsible there.

In the end, this means that decisions are made that secure the election or re-election in the short term, but in the medium to long term represent more disadvantages than advantages for future generations. It makes sense to incur debts that future generations will have to pay for in the long term, but which will be used to pay for electoral gifts in the short term. It makes sense to make decisions that only have an effect in the election period, because political opponents who govern in subsequent election periods could benefit from decisions that make sense in the long term. Moreover, despots can use the time within election periods to dispute voters' rights.

As a result, humans who prefer permanent positions do not run for politicians, even though they would be suitable and willing. Moreover, short-term decisions are encouraged among all humans because the future of the policies that affect them is uncertain. Because humans see how political leaders make decisions at the expense of future generations, they also tend to make such decisions themselves because they consider them justified. Future generations are increasingly overburdened by this because the costs can no longer be earned by them.

The solution is a new election of politicians and a change of laws as soon as a quorum is reached. A quorum is fulfilled as soon as enough those entitled to vote have cast their vote for it during an unlimited period of time. Once a quorum has been met, a meeting or voting of all those entitled to vote takes place to decide on the matter. A quorum, rather than a periodic election, makes it meaningful to make long-term decisions. If a law is good or a politician is popular, there will never be enough votes to trigger its quorum. If the opposite is the case, it can happen after just one day.

In the above example of the Minister of Education, he could not introduce project teaching as stipulated in the programme, but retains frontal teaching. This makes so many voters dissatisfied that he is deselected after three months. Those who are dissatisfied can cast their vote in the So-called deselection quorum at any time, together with the reasons for holding a new election. As soon as enough those entitled to vote do so, a new election is held for the office of that politician. To avoid this, the politician can change his behaviour or involve those entitled to vote in his decision-making. In addition, citizens can at any time demand their participation in decision-making through a So-called veto quorum. The last two ways to influence political fear-mongering are the citizens' initiative and the petition. These allow those entitled to vote to propose a particular decision and, if the majority is reached, politicians must implement it. The same applies to unpopular laws. Once they are on the statute book, they can go to the responsible minister for resubmission with a So-called repeal quorum. If the majority votes in favour, he must amend or abolish the law accordingly.

The humans learn to clearly name the triggers of their fears and to be able to take action against them. In the same way, they learn to name the triggers for joy and how they can become happy together. Through the quorums, discontent can be voiced at any time and have an impact if enough other citizens feel the same way. The action of fear no longer results in hate as a reaction, but in a vote and expression of opinion.

4.1.4 Government past the will of the people

Current democracies involve citizens either representatively or directly. In parliamentary and presidential democracies, elected representatives determine government and legislation. Citizens cannot contribute their will on an ongoing basis and cannot follow committee meetings. Direct democracies, such as in Switzerland, allow citizens to vote on proposed legislation that a minimum number of citizens do not like, and to create or amend constitutional articles. The problem with this is that citizen turnout fluctuates. If too few citizens participate, there is a risk of a minority government.

The solution is dynamic democracy. Its procedures for election of persons, legislation and government can be indirect, representative or direct. If turnout is low, no quorum is triggered and politicians can govern indirectly on their own. If turnout is too low, the participation quorum is triggered and councils govern with politicians in a representative manner. If turnout is high, quorums are triggered and citizens govern directly through committees and voting. The Ministry of State

Organisation coordinates political structures, processes and contents, especially when several ministries are involved in a project. Federal Moderators chair and moderate state policy events. This way, citizens know who is responsible and where they can participate and how.

4.1.5 Power vacuum during revolutions

In the past, the changeover to a new system usually happened through revolutions. If the revolutionaries had not prepared a concept for the time afterwards, the old rulers came back to power. If they had a new concept, it had to work immediately without having time to build the necessary structures. For example, first enough citizens must be organised in parties to know the interests of the voters and be able to represent them in a parliament or council. The more hastily concepts for new policy systems have to be built, the more prone to error they are. If citizens are not given the opportunity to recognise and correct faults, they will adapt to a flawed system.

The solution is a new system, the introduction of which allows much to remain as it is for the time being. It merely adds more possibilities that either supplement or replace the old ones. The state organisation volume assigns tasks to citizens, politicians and state employees to fulfil in political structures and processes. To allow for a gradual or sudden shift to the new system, it can be adapted to current systems. The procedures can be easily applied in families, companies, cities, states and international organisations by merely changing those entitled to vote.

For the sudden handover of power, the procedures of direct democracy are used without exception, leading to the direct election of all 18 ministers. The 18 ministers take up their work and follow the instructions of the volumes on the constitution and their ministry. The Minister of State Organisation immediately creates all the conditions for parties, quorums, committees and voting. Elections are then held for the deputy ministers. Until the deputy ministers are elected, the procedures on the state of exception and the new election and reporting in the state of emergency apply.

The gradual changeover to the new system follows the example for the Federal Republic of Germany, which is listed at the end of each ministry volume. In these, all ministries and their agencies are assigned to their new area of responsibility and conditions and measures that have become unnecessary are abolished. The new laws and constitutional articles are gradually imported as soon as the necessary majorities in parliaments, councils or referendums are in place.

4.2 Digital

The problem with digitalisation lies in its slow, uncertain and haphazardly executed nature. For private citizens, only the internet is available and not even nationwide and with sufficient speeds. The solution is a ministry that is responsible for digitalisation.

4.2.1 Obsolete analogue state system

Digitalisation in the state is insufficient for the current challenges. Much still has to be done in paper form and the offices cannot be reached digitally. The programmes and operating systems used are rarely open source and free of charge, but provide for capital export to foreigner companies, which often have to sell or keep security gaps in their systems to secret services. The same applies to digital devices. Citizens usually have to use different programmes with different access data when collaborating digitally with authorities. The internet enables the theft of data from state organs, espionage and the manipulation of opinions and election results.

When I searched the organisational charts of all German ministries during the investigation for this book, I found units or departments for digitalisation in almost all ministries. There is no central coordination and often regions and municipalities again have their own responsible offices, programmes and access data.

The solution is to create a ministry that regulates and drives digitalisation nationwide through its own intranet and matching devices. The Ministry of Digital Affairs operates a People's Innovation Company to produce people's computers and software so that citizens can make certified treaties, hold votes, organise themselves in directories and communicate with governments in all departments via the people's computer on a protected intranet. Companies can process their data, payments, industrial property rights, purchases and sales in a legally secure environment. Digitised administration can eliminate the need for paper. The Ministry of Digital Affairs can use algorithms to evaluate the data of all directories and authorities, process it statistically and simulate the future effects of policy decisions.

4.2.2 Unprotected data

Data protection is patchy and often undermined by international corporations. General Terms and Conditions allow states to use data contrary to the law in the home country of the owners. Algorithms that can control markets and opinions are insufficiently audited and not subject to democratic control.

The solution is an intranet that the country's citizens can control, a digital police force and a data protection law that puts the owners of the data at the centre. Whoever originates data is the owner of that data and can protect it from unauthorised access or release it. The digital police can be accessed on the internet and intranet via a companion application in the browser. It is supported with weapons from military cyber defence. Citizens help determine the appearance and applications on the intranet via the Feedback Directory.

4.2.3 Internet as a lawless space

The internet offers a virtually lawless space because broadcasters and recipients cannot be identified beyond doubt. Data can thus be stolen and manipulated. Criminals use the worldwide interconnection of computers and servers, which means that police forces in individual countries can no longer carry out cross-border criminal prosecution. Police presence, as in the cityscape, is non-existent on the internet. Control that enables companies and citizens to ensure the authenticity and security of their data is not possible under the conditions of the internet. The worldwide connection in the same data network with insecure terminal devices poses psychological and financial dangers for the population.

The solution is to run an intranet within the country and the internet at the same time. On the intranet, each device is assigned to a responsible citizen, making it a highly legal place, especially for children, traders and entrepreneurs. The internet remains intact and does not need to be regulated. Users are aware of the existing risks and can switch to the intranet in case of doubt.

4.3 Media

The problem with the media lies in their biased and manipulative reporting and opinion-forming. My activities in state and private film and television gave me an insight that made me aware of the current conditions and led me to the following ideas. The solution is a state-run media that is bound by the will of the voters and the law, and a free press that only has to reveal its partisan stance and is not allowed to spread lies.

4.3.1 Manipulated role models

Advertising, films, shows and documentaries create stereotypes such as role models of men and women, race, religion, age, wealth and appeal. If a role image is used in many media, a trend can emerge that promotes civic behaviour according to this role image. This management of the population is not democratically organised and can therefore be seen as manipulative at the least and biased at the most. For example, the role model of the woman who takes care of the household and children instead of earning money like the man promotes the professional model of the housewife in many families. This gives rise to the opinion among humans that this behaviour is recognised and desirable in order to be successful or not.

The solution is a media minister who can limit the dissemination of certain role models in the media as soon as the population authorises him to do so by means of a quorum and approves suitable projects in voting. The state media can be obliged by law to present balanced role models.

4.3.2 Manipulative reporting

News programmes and reports are particularly susceptible to biased and manipulative reporting. The selection of interview partners, verbal contributions and image content is usually biased. Certain parties are not asked or included. The omission and avoidance of undesirable reports deliberately influence the viewer's memory about the possible alternatives. The same applies in reverse for parties that are endorsed by the medium. They then represent the only alternative. The order of the video clips and whether there is a longer video clip or only a short word clip with a picture decides which report is stored in the memory as important or unimportant. The manipulation of facts takes place through the targeted composition of images. For example, persons who are to appear powerful are filmed from below. If a meeting is to appear well-attended, although it is not, no images from above are used, but rather filming is done at shoulder height or tilted down from above, so that the viewer can never perceive the entire surroundings around the meeting. If no number is given but, for example, "thousands" are mentioned, the actual number is to be kept secret.

Negative headlines create fear and powerlessness in the viewer, which makes a human easier to control because he seeks protection in the herd. At most, there are exceptional opportunities for viewers to participate by making donations. True to the principle: "Only bad news are good news", certain news items are included in the programme or sorted out. A few news agencies in the world support the majority of all news programmes with reports. They make a pre-selection and neglect predominantly good news. Negative headlines and So-called "uproarious topics" direct discontent specifically at certain groups of people. In this way, sections of the population can be played off against each other and incited instead of turning against the responsible politicians.

The solution is a free press that is not allowed to spread demonstrable lies, but is otherwise free in its choice of content and sources. It is different with the state press. Its content and sources depend on the lawful orders of its broadcaster. The Ministry of Media Affairs operates the state television and ensures that citizens are informed about current policies through news, documentaries and feature films. One broadcaster is responsible only for citizen participation in government. Another broadcaster provides partisan information from ministries and political parties, and another broadcaster provides impartial, unannounced and undercover reporting from ministries and their agencies. Another broadcaster films and broadcasts educational content from all state educational institutions. A broadcaster for youths prepares all topics from other broadcasters in a way suitable for youths.

4.3.3 Ideologically controlled editorial offices

The internal structure of editorial offices is hierarchical with a chief of service who approves, modifies or rejects the editors' contributions, an editor-in-chief who enforces the policy direction and the intendant who supervises everything. Intendants act on orders from the managing directors or from the Television Council. In the case of public broadcasting, the television council is responsible for its broadcasts and, in particular, influences partisan reporting in the news, which benefits the parties of its members. The fourth power in the state, namely the reporting power, is not democratically organised or controlled.

Freedom of the press and freedom of the arts make these one-sided information and filter bubbles possible. The shift to the internet makes those responsible even harder to track down because they can remain hidden somewhere abroad and in secret algorithms. There is no obligation to publish biased attitudes of a media so that consumers know what they are getting into.

The solution is to democratise the state media landscape. State broadcasters fulfil the lawful tasks of reporting and co-determination. In shows, viewers have the opportunity to participate interactively in discussions and decisions via their People's Computer. All intendants and moderators of the broadcasters are directly elected. Funding comes from tax revenues, which citizens can vote on annually. Free press is not allowed to spread false news and must publish the policy stance of its editors or reporters. As independent reporters, members of the Free Press are allowed to participate in the monitoring teams of the non-partisan state broadcaster. This state broadcaster has monitoring teams to detect violations of the law in state institutions.

4.4 Labour

The problems in labour policy are a cumbersome bureaucracy, an opaque labour market, uncertain company data, ineffective consumer protection, disadvantaged employees and an unfair pension system. These problems slow down the national economy and create international locational disadvantages. The solutions are unified management of all state institutions by the Ministry of Labour, a Labour Directory for applicants, companies and consumers, a Company Auditing Agency, democratic participation of workers, and pension models of economic forms.

4.4.1 Cumbersome bureaucracy

In state institutions, the So-called public service, there are bureaucratic hierarchical ways of working that are slow and uncoordinated. Citizens wait a long time for services or have to go from office to office to get appropriate services. Often one office does not know what the other does and who is responsible. All authorities have their own administration for personnel, digitalisation, finance and procurement. This causes costs and ties up skilled workers. Procurement is often not comprehensible for citizens and more expensive due to many individual orders.

The solution is democratic ways of working in state institutions with direct election of superiors and negotiation and voting by state employees of working plans to fulfil the law orders. The town hall is the focal point with offices of all ministries. The administration is fully digitalised and all data can be retrieved or notarised in real time. Individual administrative tasks are carried out by appropriate ministries for all ministries. For example, the Ministry of Finance is responsible for paying government personnel.

4.4.2 Opaque labour market

The labour market is opaque because graduates or unemployed people cannot see in which sectors there are currently and in the future many vacancies and for which of these jobs they have sufficient skills. Educational qualifications or further training can lead to unemployment. Companies with vacancies do not know how many workers with suitable skills are in their vicinity or at which location the number of sought-after persons is particularly high. They also cannot see how many of these skilled workers are currently unemployed or willing to change jobs. The Employment Office does not ask applicants or employers what they want and tends to provide passive support in the form of cash benefits.

The solution is a Labour Directory that shows where and when jobs become available and what requirements, achievements, activities and colleagues can be expected. Through a link to the Education Directory, all current and future graduates of the appropriate degrees in the area are displayed. By linking to the Social Directory, all job-seeking Social Villagers are displayed. Employed and unemployed people can indicate in their profile that they are looking for work in order to receive suitable job offers. All companies must report their vacancies and persons must report their job search in the Labour Directory. Application documents and invitation letters are automatically written and can be customised. The Employment Office focuses on personal advice and placement, conducts fairs and company visits, networks jobseekers and supports them in setting up businesses.

4.4.3 Insecure company data

The data on which costs and profits companies generate are insufficiently recorded and evaluated. As a result, companies can have their costs partially borne by the general public. This is referred to as So-called negative external effects. This is the case, for example, with products that have to be disposed of at a cost. Products and production methods are insufficiently tested in this respect. This leads to disadvantages for companies that bear all their costs themselves.

The solution is a Company Auditing Agency, which regularly appears with its auditors for announced and unannounced audits. The structure and procedure are similar to the initial and regular audits for cars. There are different auditors for taxes, economic key figures and rules, technical products, innovations and legality.

Digital data of companies are insufficiently protected on the internet and every company has to take its own security precautions and buy in specialised personnel. Digitalisation is endangered because companies are afraid to use the digital space for fear of criminals. That would be like forbidding children to play outside alone because there are child molesters. At the moment when a majority has to hide from a minority, politics has failed.

The solution is an intranet that guarantees companies data security and legal certainty in the digital space. Companies can send or receive data via the directories and handle all their administration, ordering, recruitment and sales via additional applications in the Labour Directory. All data from taxes, companies and machines with a source code are evaluated by algorithms to create a simulation. This simulation can be used to simulate and test future laws and launches. The security of the data remains guaranteed because the intranet is operated via its own lines, operating systems, servers and terminal devices. Registration works via the identity card, making each user as identifiable as in real life, where a notary would be present at all times.

4.4.4 Ongoing real wage reductions

Employees have had to accept real wage cuts for decades because their labour unions are unable to negotiate wage increases. On the one hand, this is because employers receive the money and only pass it on to the employee at the end of the month when they pay the wages. On the other hand, the labour unions negotiate wages for the coming year or even years. So the employers have enough time to raise prices so that the wage increase is offset by a price increase, i.e. inflation. Automation is also used to lower wages. Companies produce more and more with the same number of employees and do not adjust wages to the development of profits.

The solution is different economic forms with different wage models and opportunities for negotiation between employers and employees. Labour unions use dues to buy shares in companies in the sectors they represent to get more voting rights at general meetings.

4.4.5 Disadvantaged employees

The working environment of employees is mostly characterised by submissiveness and immaturity. Superiors order subordinates what to do and what not to do. Some humans take out their emotional frustration on their subordinates because they don't fight back for fear of losing their jobs.

The solution is a democratic work environment, which is mandatory in some economic forms. There, subordinates elect their superiors and can also deselect them. In Company Auditing Agency audits, all employees have to fill in satisfaction questionnaires and can also make suggestions for improvement. Problems are dealt with in company committees, where all those entitled to vote have a say.

Reconciling family and private life is difficult because, on the one hand, two persons in the household have to work in order to have enough money. On the other hand, children and childcare are considered a burden on the labour force, which is why parents of many children or single parents are shunned on the labour market. Those who can offer their children everything hardly see them grow up and vice versa. The solution is work models such as partner work, where partners share a job or colleagues are allowed to have partners in the colleagues. Employers' childcare services vary in scope depending on the economic form. Childcare provision from the state guarantees every child a place in childcare at all times, as all state childcare is adequately covered by child benefit.

4.4.6 Unfair pension system

The pension system is unfair for future generations. The pay-as-you-go system was developed at a time when there were more young humans than pensioners. The incentive was thus given to have few or no children, thus saving money and still receiving just as much money in retirement as humans who have raised many children who also pay a lot into the pension fund thanks to well-paid jobs. In order to give old voters gifts that politicians use to buy their votes, a large part of the pension is now financed with tax money. This money is missing for investments in the future and due to the national debt, today's generation of pensioners is living at the expense of future generations. For future generations, this means an earlier death through impoverishment in old age and a decreasing life expectancy.

The solution is a pension system in every economic form. Those who have too little pension to survive can move into the Social Village and have to work in basic supply until they die. Compensation payments from tax revenues are discontinued, as are top-ups for low pensions. The pay-as-you-go system is switched in favour of private provision in the family or commercial pension models of the four economic forms.

4.4.7 Ineffective consumer protection

Consumers know less about the products they buy than the producers. All too often, this information asymmetry is used that the quality of the product can be inferior, that it comes from countries with lower standards and that it is environmentally unsound. All this information would possibly lead customers to make a different purchase decision. Once consumers are damaged by a product, it is difficult for them to prove that the damage was caused by the product. For example, electronic products break shortly after the warranty period because wear parts were installed at key points that do not last longer. The companies aim to increase sales through inferior goods, thus damaging purchasing power and the environment.

The solution is certification of production methods and seals of approval for origin, quality and environmental protection. Company Auditing Agency auditors award such certificates and seals as part of their product audits. The Company Auditing Agency conducts consumer research into repeated complaints by consumers. Consumers can report their experiences with products in the Consumer Directory and those affected can jointly form or join consumer organisations. The Company Auditing Agency is responsible for arbitration proceedings conducted between consumer organisations and companies. Entrepreneurs must publish the test results and display them visibly on the packaging. For this purpose, there is a food traffic light, indication of origin, quality label and environmental traffic light. The Social Market Economy also offers the possibility of always complying with all the highest standards, so that consumers do not have to make an increased effort to obtain information there.

4.4.8 Finance economy without alternatives

Those who want to use their money to make more money can only join the neoliberal global finance economy. Joint-stock companies are companies that mainly help to connect the finance economy with the real economy. The real economy is used to produce and trade goods and services. The finance economy does the same with capital. It becomes problematic when the owners of a company are unknown and capital can be redistributed on the financial market to the richest investors who have the best information. This is harmful to the national economy because the profits from the creation of value with capital are spent abroad or concentrated in the hands of a few humans, although many humans were needed to create this value. For example, it is hardly possible neither to buy products from joint-stock companies nor to go to work for them, to invest money with them or to live with them for rent. A poor population in particular agrees out of necessity with the lowest prices, jobs at any wage, money investment opportunities for low amounts, and rental housing no matter what the circumstances. Shareholders profit from part of the prices, wages, trading fees and rents, which is why they do not have to go to work themselves. Owners of joint-stock companies do not live with the population that works for them and usually do not know them. Redistribution in the finance economy increases the number of poor people and decreases the number of rich people who get richer for it. This weakens purchasing power and lowers living standards, resulting in fewer profits in the long run. Individuals can hardly escape this ruinous circular economy.

The solution is joint-stock companies that must provide the names and residences of their shareholders in order to participate in the domestic economy. The general meeting of shareholders elects the board of directors and determines remuneration in a democratic and digital process. Further requirements are imposed by the ministries of economy, ensuring alternative financial markets in which joint-stock companies that are more socially or liberally minded participate. Investors, consumers, employees and tenants are given several alternatives where they can invest, earn or spend their money. Different stock exchanges make it possible to invest money in the different economic forms.

4.4.9 Blind Financial Supervisory Authority

The state Financial Supervisory Authority has insufficient information to effectively detect crimes in the financial market. The criminals can steal or obtain money through accounts and companies abroad, So-called letterbox companies, without it being possible to check them. Even if cases become known, there is little leverage because auditors, police officers, public prosecutors and judges cannot investigate and judge worldwide. How solvent a company really is is something that private rating agencies and economic auditors usually only investigate and disclose to those who pay them. For example, banks package loans of solvent and insolvent companies into a fund and market it as solvent. Stockbrokers can do the same with indices and joint-stock companies. Informed investors then forgo these financial products, while uninformed retail investors suffer the losses.

The solution is state supervision for banks, stock exchanges and insurance companies, whose head is directly elected. Citizens can petition him and consumers can demand information. A state rating agency checks the solvency of all domestic companies using data from the Company Auditing Agency. Foreigner companies are only audited if fees are deducted for buying securities. Only solvent companies are granted stock exchange listing and the share prices show the performance of the company and the share.

4.4.10 Environmentally damaging agriculture

The problem with today's agriculture is that it damages the environment more than it benefits it. Particularly problematic are fallow soils that are only covered with vegetation for a short part of the year and, moreover, only at low growth. Annual plants at low growth store little CO_2 and consume more land than necessary. Such soil is not able to store water and nutrients for long. Therefore, it is fertilised and irrigated. The fertiliser contaminates the drinking water and the irrigation reduces the drinking water reserves for humans. Monocultures of plants and animals attract pests and keep beneficial insects away. Therefore, they have to be treated with toxins or medicines. Residues that cannot be degraded accumulate in the food chain and ultimately in the human body. Pesticides lead to the extinction of insects that convert biomass and pollinate plants. Medicines produce resistant pathogens that can kill humans because no medicine is effective any more. Fallow land can produce less food than possible. Irrigation, fertilisation and pesticides raise the price of food. The exploitation of forests for timber and arable land is only made necessary by such agriculture. This reduces the air's support for oxygen and water and increases its dryness and CO_2 content. This jeopardises the usual flow of air and its content of water and heat. Weather extremes such as droughts, fires and floods are on the increase. Fishing grounds are already extensively exploited, which is why algae and jellyfish can become a plague. Genetically modified animals and plants can enter the environment and cause as yet unknown long-term effects.

The solution is to separate agriculture into indoor and outdoor. Indoors, monocultures can grow that are artificially supported with water, light and nutrients and can be genetically manipulated. Their circuits are closed so that water is treated, light is generated by renewable energy sources on the building and nutrients are produced for each other by suitably matched animals and plants. In outdoor fields, farmers practise permaculture with harvesting robots or volunteers. The fields are cultivated with a humanly assembled ecosystem that supports itself. The deliberate use of specific plants and animals in a specific place at a specific time shapes each soil to suit its condition and weather. The mixed vegetation of annual and perennial plants ensures better use of the area through the gain in height. The three-dimensional space is better used, which increases the yield. Fertilisation is provided by plants shedding their leaves and by animals through their excretions. The roots are no longer destroyed by digging, but store water or fetch it from the depths. Poisons and medicines are replaced by animals and plants that hunt pests or have healing ingredients. Permaculture is practised in fields, forests and water. Scientific studies explore what types of animals and plants are needed to create a self-sustaining ecosystem for a particular region. Successful research increasingly increases the yield by increasing the growth of healthy animals and plants.

4.5 Economy

The problems in economic policy lie in the world-wide monopoly of the no-alternative neoliberal global market economy as the only available economic form, an unnatural economy, a dwindling middle class and risky economic fluctuations on the world market. The problems in social policy lie in the worldwide competition for the lowest non-wage labour costs and for admission to existing welfare states. Social welfare is useless as a cash benefit because money cannot meet the problems of the needy. The communist planned economy offers no alternative because it does not take demand and inventiveness into account and, as the only economic form in a country, it cannot survive on the world market.

The solution is an economic policy that operates four economic forms simultaneously in one country that complement each other. This removes the dichotomy of freedom and security because citizens decide for themselves how freely or securely they want to consume and work. Social policy is conducted with the help of a democratised Planned Economy, which eliminates the subsidy of tax money or non-wage labour costs through compulsory contributions. Jobs, social welfare provision and foreign trade are only possible with foreigners if domestic supply is assured. Only the Free Market Economy can participate in the world market almost without restrictions.

4.5.1 Monopoly of an economic form

The fourth central fault in the policy system lies in the monopoly of one economic form, namely the neoliberal global market economy. The consequence is that competition between economic forms is absent. Both the state economy and its budget, as well as the private economy, are bound by the laws of the free market, the So-called invisible hand. This law states that supply and demand in free competition determine the prices at which labour, money and products are traded. As long as demand is sufficient, a corresponding supply will be found. The neoliberal global market economy uses the limitless possibilities for the circulation of money to extract money from national economies via the financial market. This is done through dividends from shares, interest from government and corporate bonds, rents from real estate and price increases in commodities that are as scarce as possible. The Central Banks increase the money supply and thus create inflation. Since most states are in debt, inflation lowers their debt burden and expropriates savers. International investors invest in shares and bonds whose dividends or interest rates are higher than the inflation rate of the respective states and their currencies. The end result is that the money supply decreases in the big countries and increases in island states known as tax havens or tax havens. In the big countries, increasingly both parents and sometimes also children have to work so that the family can survive well under the circumstances. Often, several island states host the same persons who have most of the money in the world. These persons live in several places and spend only a small part of their money there. As a result, there is no improvement in the living conditions of the inhabitants of the island states. Due to the shortage of money, goods and services have to be so cheap that residents can still survive. The super-rich benefit particularly from these low prices. Savers are treated differently depending on the size of their assets. High assets benefit from low trading fees and well-informed, trained and equipped staff. Low assets are usually invested by the savers themselves or looked after by a person who has completed vocational training or perhaps a degree in economics. The bottom line is that lower assets on the financial market suffer losses more often than higher assets. Since on the financial market, through betting, the profits of some investors can mean the losses of others, there is a redistribution between savers. This state of affairs becomes particularly problematic when the redistribution of money creates a market power that can manipulate consumers and prices. This can be done, for example, by constant advertising or by buying up companies or commodities. When this market power then makes use of the law of the richer in international anarchy, it is above all state laws. There are no international laws or agencies to regularisation what is economically allowed or prohibited. Accordingly, there can be no criminal prosecution by an international police and justice system. For example, companies can have their products manufactured by child labour and still sell the products in a country where child labour is prohibited.

The solution is to have four economic forms running simultaneously in one country, which also complement each other. In this way, they form a stable economic system that supports itself in a circular economy. The economic forms already known are used, namely the Barter Economy, Planned Economy, Social Market Economy and Free Market Economy. The almost unrestricted participation in the neoliberal global market economy is only possible in the Free Market Economy. All other economic forms only engage in foreign trade if the same standards apply abroad. Citizens have the election whether they prefer to live free and poor in the forest close to nature and exchange products, to fulfil their basic needs safely and poorly in a village solidarity community, to be safe and rich in a social entrepreneurial community or to become free and rich as a successful entrepreneur on the world market. Those who fail to get rich and become poor in the Free Market Economy and Social Market Economy can start again in the Barter Economy and Planned Economy without fear of starving, dying of thirst or freezing to death. Consumers, investors, entrepreneurs, workers and tenants have the choice of goods, services, financial products, locations, jobs and real estate in one of the economic forms. The ministries of economy ensure that their economic form is as attractive and cost-covering as possible and secure it with their own currency. The Ministry of Labour ensures smooth and equitable transitions of capital, goods, services and companies between the economic forms.

4.5.2 Dwindling middle class

Due to the competitive advantages of international corporations, medium-sized companies cannot keep up with world market prices or are split up in the course of inheritance between the generations of a family business or are bought up entirely by corporations. Privately run retailers are disappearing in city centres and department stores are springing up on the outskirts, their shops run by various chains. They advertise and pursue costly marketing strategies to retain customers with psychological tricks. Private retailers cannot keep up with this because they do not make as much turnover. Their revenues are not enough to do advertising for their shop comparable to the reach of a corporation's advertising.

The solution is a People and Ideas Stock Exchange where

medium-sized companies can raise money from the citizens of their region to grow their business. The Social Market Economy specialises in medium-sized companies and enables them to benefit from similar opportunities as large corporations. As inheritance tax only applies while debt reduction is ongoing, the intergenerational transition will not be so costly that a medium-sized company has to be sold. The Labour Directory enables companies to advertise and market themselves to their target group on the intranet. This service is only paid for as soon as profits are made.

4.5.3 Economy away from nature

The economy is highly technological, so that individuals can no longer trace value chains and production methods, and consumers can no longer repair their products. Plastics, medicines and machines are sometimes capable of doing more damage to humanity than good. Humans who would like to live close to nature have hardly any legal or adequate possibility to do so. Old ways of living to build, feed or support themselves medically are forgotten and are not developed further or integrated into the modern economy. Natural growth is disregarded and replaced by artificial growth. Artificial growth today mostly consumes finite raw materials that were only created by millions of years of natural growth. This is why humanity consumes more than can grow back. This means that humanity cannot survive.

The solution is innovative economic cycles whose growth rate is adapted to natural growth. Increasing understanding of natural growth cycles, in which millions of animal and plant species are involved, can promote natural growth. The artificial assembly of natural ecosystems is being researched, practised and improved in agriculture, barter economy and planned economy. For example, citizens can live in the forest without synthetics and pay their taxes in kind or forestry labour. Natural remedies and self-sufficiency agriculture are used in the Barter Economy and Planned Economy to ensure basic supply.

4.5.4 Social dumping

There is a race between states to have the lowest non-wage labour costs and thus the lowest social benefits. On the other hand, there is a pull effect of poverty refugees who relocate only because of the social benefits. The lowering of social standards and the exploitation of the welfare state by foreigners who never paid in taxes or contributions in the past increasingly reduces social benefits and secures future generations worse than the present.

The solution is a social market economy which, as a Social Market Economy with compulsory insurance, is open to all residents and which, as a Planned Economy, only guarantees unconditional basic security to domestic nationals at all times. As soon as foreign states implement the same economic forms or make compensation payments, foreigners can also enjoy unconditional social benefits. Restrictions on guest work and entry fees into economic forms for foreigners prevent the exploitation of the welfare state. Tariffs and restrictions on imports or exports prevent the exploitation of other states, which keeps poverty refugees out. The prohibition of subsidised exports prevents the destruction of markets in developing countries.

4.5.5 Useless social welfare

Social welfare is financial support for low wages because the poor can supplement their income with tax money. Unemployment assistance, social welfare and pensions are mainly financed by non-wage labour costs, especially wage tax, pension, unemployment, health and long-term care insurance. It also makes up a large part of the overall budget. Thus the employees bear the costs of irresponsible labour market policies of the employers. This particularly benefits foreign corporations and investors who withdraw their profits from the country and, as soon as the country becomes too impoverished, settle in new countries and market their products or invest money there. Therefore, share prices of corporations can rise even though they lay off employees en masse. The long-term unemployed are given money for living expenses and housing. In return, they have to take measures they don't really want. They get used to a life regulated by others in shame because they belong to the lower class.

The solution is Planned Economy social welfare. Humans who work in the field of social welfare tend to be left-wing and not averse to the idea of a community of solidarity with Planned Economy. All welfare recipients live in Social Villages, where they get to know each other, receive concentrated state social benefits in kind and earn their own living. The state already owns many plots of land that are built on with habitable buildings. Barracks are particularly suitable for this because they have buildings for food and health as well as an existing supply network for supplies. This saves the state an immense amount of money. Firstly, barracks can be used flexibly in different ways in peacetime and wartime, which means that profits or benefits are constantly generated from maintenance costs. Second, with common rooms, expensive devices for cooking and laundry are shared. Third, all social services are pooled in one place, eliminating costs of travel, administration and overlap. Fourth, the Planned Economy creates a basic supply that Social Villagers earn in compulsory working hours, thus not burdening the state budget. Fifth, the Planned Economy creates profits. Through further training in the Education Centre, the human capital of the inhabitants increases. Planned Enterprises produce products that the state would otherwise have to order, thus encouraging profits in certain private enterprises. The unemployed can finance their luxury supply themselves. Accordingly, their free time away from compulsory working hours decreases and the supply of products increases, but does not burden the state budget. Start-ups from the Planned Economy are able to conquer the world market through lower market entry costs. This economic development is self-financing through funds into which successful companies pay that were once founded using money from the fund. Founding members and employees are easy to find because they live near each other and know that they all have enough time and education. Through the Social Village Directory, anyone can search for suitable residents in the Social Villages to form groups. The prerequisite is that a resident has released his or her visibility for the search function.

4.5.6 Flawed communist planned economy

The problem with the communist planned economy was that it was managed dictatorially by the single party. Workers could not be inventive or become entrepreneurs and customers could not obtain desired products. The fault with the communist planned economy was that the government determined the supply and not the inhabitants the demand.

The solution is a planned economy with an annual vote on demand and an algorithm that continuously adjusts supply to current demand, because all services are billed digitally with a card and the digital currency working hours. The advantage of this type of Planned Economy is that it works together with the market economy. It uses the waste from the market economy, reuses it, repairs it or upgrades it and sells it again in the market economy. It catches the unemployed from the market economy, trains them and ensures that they can re-enter the labour market of the Social Market Economy or Free Market Economy as more capable employees or entrepreneurs. The welfare state can be saved by switching to minimum benefits in kind in the Social Village and creating a booster effect by marketing technical innovations from the people. This provides social security and creates employment. The state generates profits to finance the reforms and national solidarity is achieved through the help of the population to advance hope and integration.

4.5.7 Risky cyclical fluctuations in the global economy

The global economy carries the risk that a global economic downturn can lead to rising prices, unemployment rates and national debt everywhere. Recent examples include the financial crisis from 2008, the Corona pandemic from 2020 and the war in Europe from 2022. Global supply chains for money, goods, services and personnel cause prices to fall when there is a surplus and to rise when there is a shortage. Localised wars, natural disasters and policy failures in individual countries can have an impact on many other countries.

The solution is a shielding but not a sealing off from the world economy. Four economic forms that are separate from each other and regions or countries that can support themselves will create sufficient independence. Any world trade is a gain in luxury, but not essential. The Barter Economy and Planned Economy may only export surpluses that do not endanger the regenerative capacity of their habitats and the basic supply of their inhabitants. The Social Market Economy has downturn insurance and the Ministry of Finance operates a fund to compensate for economic cycles. Additional tax revenues are saved during an upswing and paid out again during a downturn. The Free Market Economy can therefore compete internationally with low taxes and requirements without affecting the rest of the population. Only those who knowingly and willingly participate in the Free Market Economy expose themselves to the risk of total loss or dependency.

4.6 Finance

The problems in fiscal policy lie in the indebted national budget, an overly complicated tax system, the expropriating central bank policy and the export of capital to tax havens through the international financial market. I got to know the machinations of the international financial market while working at the Frankfurt Stock Exchange. I had the opportunity for insightful background discussions with analysts to develop the following solutions. The solution is a democratised fiscal policy with an annual budget vote, elected head of the Central Bank, four economic forms with their own currencies and business taxes, and a People's Bank for the domestic financial market.

4.6.1 Indebted states

Countries that spend more money than they earn go into debt. They usually do this on the international financial market and not with their own inhabitants. As with any loan, borrowing fees are due in the form of debt interest. If the recipients of the interest on the debt are abroad, this money flows out of the national economy and into other countries, where it is spent and strengthens the purchasing power there. This makes poor countries poorer and increasingly dependent on international investors. Whoever holds the majority of the debts in a state has the greatest influence on the politicians there and can blackmail them with a state bankruptcy. Because not only one level in the state is indebted, but all municipalities, cities, regions and the nation, investors have many gateways to assert their claims to power.

The solution is for the state to lend money only from its citizens, and if that is not enough, to stop spending. The debts abroad are paid off by debts at home. The existing debts are paid off through taxes on land, inheritances and gifts, so that the originating generations pay for their debts and do not burden future generations with them.

4.6.2 Unfair fiscal equalisation

Some parts of the country can take in more than they spend, others less. Through financial equalisation, the strong support the weak parts of the country. If this support becomes permanent, efficient, resourceful or thrifty politicians and citizens are punished and lazy, bored or wasteful politicians and citizens are rewarded.

The solution is an annual budget vote in which citizens vote on spending. In financial plans, all ministries draw up their wishes on how they want to use the revenues saved. Because the budget is saved for the coming year, no more can be distributed than has been saved. In emergency situations, the savings for the coming year can be tapped. For municipalities that consistently take in less per capita, the Company Auditing Agency's business consultants can propose measures and the people can adjust the affected municipality's policy on revenues and expenditure through a quorum.

4.6.3 Complicated tax system

The tax system is so complicated that it takes many tax officials to check all tax assessments and even that is only possible on a random basis. At the same time, a profession of tax consultants is establishing itself. Only the rich can afford tax consultants, so the poor tend to pay too much tax because they don't know the savings models. Tax consultants and tax officials are well-trained professionals who waste their skills on an unnecessary activity.

The solution is a simple tax system that taxes only added value and companies. Value added tax is the same throughout the country. Business taxes vary depending on the economic form. In the Free Market Economy and Barter Economy they are the lowest and turnover is taxed. In the Social Market Economy and Planned Economy they are highest and profits are taxed. Substance is only taxed if there are debts. The settlement of the tax is fully automated via tax accounts. In this process, a tax account is switched between the broadcaster and the recipient of a payment, where the amount is only held for a very short time in order to deduct the tax from it. An algorithm detects anomalies and citizens can report suspected tax fraud. The Tax Investigation Department then examines these allegations.

4.6.4 Uncoordinated state banks

The many different state-owned banks offer a non-transparent variety of offers, sometimes identical offers. They employ a large number of board members and staff, although all banks do similar business.

The solution is a state bank that takes over all these services and enables all citizens to have a free account. Money transactions between citizens and the state, such as the issuing of government bonds or loans for business start-ups, are carried out through this bank.

4.6.5 Central Banks in the currency war

Since the financial crisis in 2008, the Central Banks of the state currencies have continued to print money. In doing so, they increase the money supply without giving anything in return. This devalues the currencies, they lose value and the savers who hold their assets in money are expropriated. This always happens when the interest rates on monetary assets at the bank are lower than the inflation rate. For example, if the Central Bank's key interest rate is 0% and the inflation rate is 2%, all humans who have cash in their wallets or bank accounts lose 2% of that every year. Only the rich can escape this because they have so much money that they can buy securities from unnecessary cash. Those who are not familiar with securities trading are putting their savings at risk. Those who have enough money buy the necessary information and services and do not lose anything, but gain.

Actually, currency devaluation is an insidious means to have cheaper prices on the world market and thus take business away from other countries. Therefore, a currency war developed in which the Central Banks of most countries all devalued their currencies. Different ways were chosen to achieve this. Sometimes by buying foreign currency, sometimes by printing more banknotes, sometimes by buying securities in the form of shares and bonds. Even worthless loans from insolvent companies and states were bought by the Central Banks at the expense of the taxpayers. This damage weighs heavily on future generations, because the indebtedness of the states and the expropriation of the majority of the population reduces the financial room for manoeuvre for coming challenges.

The solution is a directly elected head of the Central Bank. The Central Bank's task is to achieve price stability despite full employment. To fulfil this task, it is supported by one Note-issuing Bank for each of the four ministries of economy. Thus, the Central Bank is responsible for monetary policy and exchange rates, the Note-issuing Banks for currency policy. The use of fiscal resources is not necessary because there are currency reserves. If they are depleted, another economic form takes over until there are again sufficient values that can be deposited as collateral. In case of doubt, the country closes itself off from the world market, leaving many companies in the Free Market Economy to go bankrupt and investors to suffer a total loss. The other economic forms absorb the affected population by increasing their sales to support them. The Central Bank and the Note-issuing Banks set a key interest rate that corresponds to the inflation rate. Through the People's Bank, it is paid out to savers so that their financial assets are not expropriated. On the contrary, an interest rate equal to the growth of the Gross Domestic Product is paid out so that citizens are motivated to create and maintain value together.

4.6.6 International financial markets create impoverishment

Securities not only contain value, they also create added value. For example, shares contain part of the value of a company. This value is stated in the price of the share. The added value is the share's dividend, which is distributed to shareholders as a share in profits. Bonds contain the value of the loan to a company or a state. This value is stated in the price of the bond. The added value is the interest that has to be paid regularly for the borrowed money for a certain term. All these values and surplus values contain an equivalent value that can be found in the real economy. Companies consist of buildings, material and personnel, states of authorities, infrastructure, taxpayers and voters. Entrepreneurs, employees and citizens want growth that enables them to live equally good or better lives. Growth is not always money, but rather happiness, which everyone understands differently. Money has the purpose of being able to secure the future, because action potential can be stored in it. For money to enter this financial system, there must be humans who want to give their savings for the growth of companies and states in order to increase their assets with the added value. This can be for old-age provision or because people want more and more money. It becomes problematic when this investment aid for the economy turns into an object that is bet on and the purpose of the economic aid is displaced by pure monetary gain.
A speculative value is the price difference between buying

and selling a security. The financial market consumes a lot of money by buying and selling only to generate profits from this value. But because there is no countervalue behind it, there must always be a loser in this transaction. The profits of one are the losses of another. A large number of securities traders, So-called day traders, own securities for only milliseconds, a day or a week. In doing so, they drive prices of securities up or down based on their expectation of a future falling or rising price. They try to base their expectations on luck or the best possible information. This causes fluctuations because the future is uncertain. Those who want to bring certainty into their future expectations must be in a position to help determine the future. This creates an incentive to blackmail politicians after owning the majority of their debts, or to blackmail managers after owning the majority of their company's shares.

The financial system disadvantages humans with little money and favours those with a lot. On the one hand, there are fees for every purchase, which are lower when a lot is bought. On the other hand, the rich can determine prices through the mass of securities. If they hold back a lot of securities, the supply falls below the demand and the price rises. If they suddenly sell many of the same securities, the price falls. Because there are also securities for food and energy, a population can suffer from a price increase and afford less. In the worst case, humans starve or freeze to death because of this. So those who only look at the profit when investing money and not whether they are causing famine or wars with it, are causing costs with their profits that they are not bearing. Because the profiteers rarely live in the countries where they invest their money, they do not have to suffer or witness their effects. The richer an investor is, the less important the common good of those affected by his investments becomes to him, because he can no longer keep track of all those to whom he lends money. The service providers of these investors are securities traders. They carry out securities trading on a grand scale in banks, investment banks or asset managers on stock exchanges all over the world. They impoverish the world's population for the benefit of the world's richest humans. This is done by having joint-stock companies that distribute their profits to persons who do not live in the country and spend the money there again. This outflow of money reduces purchasing power. The Gross Domestic Product of a country can be used as a yardstick. There are states in the world that do not expel any Gross Domestic Product, for example Monaco or the Cayman Islands. It is striking that all these states are known as So-called tax havens. The assets of the world's population are redistributed there. If these states were to publish their Gross Domestic Product, it would be unusually high for states with a small area and few inhabitants.

For example, there are 10 globally trading asset managers, one of which is called Black Rock. Each asset manager raises money from retail investors through automated exchange-traded funds (ETFs), and from large investors through personal advice, informational advantages and responsible politicians and managers in key positions. With this money, asset managers buy 10% of all shares in the biggest and most powerful companies in every country in the world. This means that all asset managers own all the most powerful joint-stock companies. Asset managers themselves are also joint-stock companies. Each asset manager owns 10% of the other asset managers. This means that the asset managers own themselves and are thus increasingly bundling the world's assets with themselves. Because the law of the rich applies on the international financial market, a world power can be built up that is not elected, operates in secret and is able to take advantage of the damage done to others because it does not have to bear the costs of the consequences.

The solution is to give the population the opportunity to disconnect from this financial system by having each economic form have its finance economy. Only the finance economy of the Free Market Economy participates in the international financial market. The Social Market Economy only does so if all participants comply with social standards so that there is no cost to the general public. The Planned Economy and Barter Economy do not do it at all. The People's Bank creates a domestic stock exchange, the So-called People's Stock Exchange. All securities traded there are domestic and can only be bought or sold by nationals who have a savings account with the People's Bank. Securities for commodities, food, energy and weapons cannot be bought there. Residents of the country can use them to invest in the growth of their state, which they themselves manage democratically. Purchasing power increases, which also benefits the Free Market Economy and with it the international financial market. So that not only the state and existing companies can use the savers' money to grow or improve, but also inventors and founders, there is the Ideas Stock Exchange. Both exchanges are independent of the international financial market because only domestic citizens use the money saved at home, use it to improve the domestic economy and spend the profits from the improvements back at home. This circuit promotes rising living standards. Only 10% of the total assets on these state-run exchanges can also be bought by foreigners through a foreign fund and traded on the international financial market.

4.7 Innovation

The problems with innovation lie firstly in the corporate culture, which is dominated by large corporations for outdated technologies, secondly in the inadequate opportunities to develop, learn about and buy innovations and thirdly in the inadequate state protection of innovations. The solution is: first, a criminal law for procrastination of innovation; second, directories, exchanges and funds for ideas; and third, innovation auditors and industrial property rights for any kind of innovation.

4.7.1 Market power of obsolete technologies

The problem with obsolete technology is that companies have become so rich with it that they can dominate policies and markets to prevent new technologies from replacing their products. Corporations are large companies that include several companies that produce and sell in several countries. They often control entire value chains when they own companies that extract raw materials, process them into products and sell them to end customers. Thus they receive all the profits that arise in all parts of the value chain. They can set the price lower than almost any other supplier in order to force competitors out of the market. If they have no competitors or agree on prices as a cartel, they can raise the price and increase their profits. An example of such a corporation is the Shell oil company. It owns oil rigs, refineries and petrol stations.

Corporations are linked with other corporations in associations and engage in political lobbying and determine the market. A dominant position occurs when a corporation is the market leader or several corporations collude and form a So-called oligopoly. Whoever dominates the market can determine the quantities and prices of goods sold on that market. For example, there are a few oil companies that operate many petrol stations worldwide. They are connected in the association of the oil industry and ensure laws that do not hinder their business model but promote it. Their lobbyists regularly visit politicians and organise events to which they invite politicians to make them feel important and powerful. Lobbyists of environmental organisations are not so numerous and rarely visit politicians to put forward their interests. This is because an environmental organisation does not make profits, like corporations, which it could invest in paying lobbyists. Moreover, lobbyists from environmental organisations also tend to come with bad news. Then politicians tend to feel incompetent and accused. Lobbyists for new technologies do not exist because inventors are neither organised in an association nor do they have the money to hire lobbyists for a product that is not yet for sale.

Currently, corporations earn a lot of money with outdated technologies because customers do not get admission to newer technologies. Competitors who want to offer new technologies have high initial costs, the So-called market entry costs, and few revenues. Entry costs are, for example, building production facilities or renting sales space. Therefore, their prices need to be high to cover these costs. Corporations with outdated technologies can offer a product with the same benefits to consumers at a much lower price and advertise it widely. Because corporations also have a lot of leeway to lower their prices, they can lower the revenues of newcomers to the market by lowering their prices, who then can no longer pay their entry costs and disappear from the market again. For example, Shell could not provide charging facilities for electric cars at its petrol stations so that there is a nationwide supply network only for cars with internal combustion engines. This is in Shell's interest because they do not want to produce electricity but sell their extracted and refined oil. Market entry costs would be low if electric cars had an exchangeable battery that is changed at existing filling stations. This would allow electric cars to be charged as quickly as cars with internal combustion engines are refuelled. Instead, they increase market entry costs by requiring new filling stations to be built in the form of charging stations or purchased by owners of an electric car.

It also becomes problematic when corporations with outdated technologies buy up industrial property rights or young companies of innovations and prevent them from marketing in order to be able to continue marketing their outdated technology. For example, Shell could buy out a manufacturer of batteries for private homes and still continue to market heating oil with more money.

The solution is a penal code for procrastination of innovation, opportunities to create Innovation Enterprises and a way for corporations with outdated technology to invest in research and development of new technology. Procrastination of innovation means knowing about new technologies that are cheaper and less burdensome to the public, but not using them to change or even prevent production. Preventing means increasing market entry costs through market power or buying up industrial property rights in order not to be able to market them and thus prohibit marketing. Lobbying becomes public through the Lobby Directory and all lobbyists are heard on an equal footing through a fixed time allotment for appointments and events with politicians.

Market entry costs are reduced to near zero through the Innovation Enterprise start-up process. In Social Villages, founders receive buildings, tools and staff without having to pay for them. Profit-sharing to employees and taxes on profits are costs that only arise when profits are made. Procurement of materials is organised through the Procurement Office and financed through the Innovation Fund. All successful Innovation Enterprises that once received money from this fund pay into the Innovation Fund. As soon as the Innovation Enterprise has marketed its products in any economic form and country and has thus earned sufficient profits to be able to pay the market entry costs of the economic form of its election, it must leave the Social Village and procure buildings, tools, materials and personnel itself.

Corporations with obsolete technology can participate in the development of new technologies that affect their products, production methods or industry through the Research Cost Fund in the Research Directory. They can find, finance and buy existing inventions via the Ideas Directory. This enables them to be the first company on the world market to sell more or at a lower price thanks to a new technology. The risk of in-house research and development is the high cost of specialised personnel and materials. Companies gain admission to researchers, inventors, laboratories and factories for prototypes through the Ideas Directory and the Research Directory. There they can publish orders for research and development projects. The existing state educational institutions, research institutes and Think Tanks serve as voluntary service providers. They choose orders themselves and receive their wages for fulfilling them. The innovation auditors of the Company Auditing Agency check whether there are new innovations that could fit the company they are auditing. With an Innovation Database, they authenticate new innovations in companies, find suitable fields of application and successful applications, and can also offer innovations to suitable companies at the request of the inventors.

4.7.2 Partisan professors and studies

Research is not free because chairs that do not fit into the current system are not created or are abolished. For example, I studied economics and attended seminars at the planned economy chair, which was abolished shortly afterwards. Instead, more chairs of market economy were created. The allocation of chairs must be politically or financially wanted. Politicians want professors who tell the same story as the politicians and prefer their studies or create institutes for them. Business associations want professors who communicate their business and do not publish findings that are harmful to business. In return, they finance researchers and chairs who confirm the dubiousness of their products or the dubiousness of competing products in studies. If these studies are not in their favour, funding and orders are given to obedient scientists.

The solution is chairs that are assigned according to the democratically created curriculum. Ministries have their own research institutes that are supported with faculty from the colleges and can commission studies there. Universities are state colleges with all subject areas and provide different perspectives for the same studies. Faculty members are directly elected by the members of the educational institution, rated and, if necessary, deselected by quorum. Independent studies of all products are conducted by the Company Auditing Agency on a regular basis at review meetings and in long-term studies.

4.7.3 Unfree research

Researchers are not free because they often work for a professor who then claims their research results for himself or promotes or suppresses them as he sees fit. The application of researchers for state research funds takes a long time, examines risks more than benefits and takes a long time before the first funds are paid. It is also temporary and not linked to success or failure. Researchers can only decide what kind of research they do by choosing their employer. There is often competition for the first discovery and therefore data is not shared or duplicated, which is expensive, time-consuming and, in the case of experiments on animals and humans, causes unnecessary damage. The free exchange of researchers is therefore not possible, nor is the free sharing of research in order to obtain new knowledge and developments as quickly as possible. Basic research is neglected because money cannot be earned immediately. As a result, however, future innovations are less and less likely to be truly novel because they are based on new findings. Research projects for structural change in energy and transport are not coordinated and insufficiently supported with personnel, material and money.

The solution is research projects that are published in a Research Directory, where all participants are listed and linked to the findings they have found. Funding is provided by Research Cost Funds, which are sometimes endowed by the state, sometimes by companies and sometimes by voluntary private individuals. Principals can choose researchers and institutes, and researchers can choose orders and institutes or advertise orders themselves for funding or execution. The funding is linked to the requirements set by the researchers and therefore pays for the project until it is completed without any time limit until a new application is made. Through the alliance between research institutions and educational institutions, a division of labour becomes possible, leading to faster results on a larger data base. If the population decides in favour of a priority area, all professionally qualified pupils, students, teachers and state-employed researchers can conduct research on a priority area until the desired findings are achieved. To this end, the Ministry of Innovation establishes state research projects and funds research that advances these projects. Basic research is part of all educational institutions and is integrated into the curriculum. Researching companies will be obliged to use a share of personnel and material for basic research or to send them for a limited period of time for this purpose. In addition, it will be possible for voluntary citizens to engage in research in their free time. For this purpose, there is the People's Innovation Company Think Tank and the Innovation Labs. There, volunteers find other like-minded people and gain admission to premises and materials to implement their own or other people's research projects. Through innovation, humanity should be able to afford the luxury of satisfying its needs without burdening nature.

4.7.4 Insufficient protection of new ideas

The worldwide registration of an industrial property right is currently time-consuming and expensive. Many patent and trademark offices in different countries turn an invention into a cheap mass product in one country because it is not protected there, and into an expensive rarity in another country. Filing patents worldwide is too expensive for most inventors, and litigation in many countries at the same time can bankrupt them, even though they would get justice in court. Inventors have to deal with constraints on secrecy, composition and formulation that they are not initially aware of. From the idea to the appropriate industrial property right to its commercialisation is a long road on which many inventors fail, even though they have made a groundbreaking invention. Certain ideas, such as TV show formats or business processes, are not eligible for protection, even though they incur costs for research and development and could earn a lot of money by being marketed. Appropriate expert advice is expensive to obtain and you need to know how and where to get it.

The solution is an Innovation Agency that supports inventors from the idea to the product. Inventors only have to pay for this service when their idea generates profits. The Ideas Directory is a database for all industrial property rights ever filed and a digital platform where inventors, investors, employees and customers can find each other. Inventors are guided there on how to provide what information about their idea in order to create a profile and apply for an industrial property right. The rest is done by an algorithm that automatically searches for similar industrial property rights, indicates whether they are too similar, suggests suitable industrial property rights for ideas and who could be a possible customer, employee, provider or investor. The Patent Office maintains the Ideas Directory and advises inventors before they apply for industrial property rights. Patent Office auditors report breakthrough inventions with the potential for profitable global commercialisation to the Innovation Agency, which initiates the formation of a People's Innovation Company. People's Innovation Companies are companies owned by the people that produce protected innovations and sell them on a large scale worldwide at a monopoly price until the validity of the industrial property right ends. The profits are used to replace taxpayers' money.

4.8 Education

The problems in education policy affect learners and teachers in all types of schools. Learners are mostly underage students who are exposed to the arbitrariness of the teachers. Teachers are mostly academics who are exposed to the arbitrariness of the curriculum and the upper level of administration. The administration of the education system is hierarchical and bureaucratic, which means that they are not oriented towards students, teachers and companies, but towards the requirements of administrators who are subordinate to politicians.

The solution is an education policy that involves participants as young as ten years old, as well as learners, teachers, training providers, companies and research institutions.

4.8.1 Incapacitated pupils

Students experience learning as a compulsion and rarely understand the meaning and connection of and between learning contents. It is possible to achieve good grades through rote learning and without a deeper understanding. The curiosity and playfulness to understand things is trained away in favour of unquestioning obedience to a plan that comes from people one does not know and that one has to execute with humans one cannot choose. Compulsory schooling for minors becomes a problem when it forcibly parents children to immaturity. Pupils experience learning from a victim role and are not informed about their rights that could free them from this. They experience that teachers can force them to do things they do not want to do without knowing the meaning. They are graded by teachers but cannot grade teachers. They are sometimes bullied by their teachers and do not know who to turn to who is in a position of power above the teacher and independent of the educational institution. The Education

Authority, with its staff and psychologists, offers such a body, but pupils are not aware of it, let alone the prescribed complaints channel. If they are annoyed by fellow pupils, they can turn to the teacher and hope that this will lead to improvement. In the schoolyard, the law of the jungle often prevails, which is why blackmail, theft, assault, coercion and slander are too often the order of the day. Students have no influence on who is in their class, what lesson times they have, which teacher they have in which subject and how they want to learn which knowledge and when.

The solution is to democratise learning at state educational institutions. What is to be learned is defined in the curriculum. This is formulated publicly by the ministries of education, business and innovation with representatives from associations of business and science and presented to the affected learners and teachers for voting. Pupils decide how they want to learn by choosing courses at the beginning of a learning year and thus compiling their timetable. Compulsory education means spending a minimum number of hours per week in courses. Few courses have to be taken because their knowledge is essential for survival in today's society. Many courses can be freely chosen so that learners can discover their talents and interests. Mostly, unpopular but unavoidable knowledge can be learnt in popular courses through projects where it has to be applied for a change. This increases the willingness to learn knowledge that is not so easy to apply. Late risers and early birds are free to choose their own teaching times, as courses are offered at different times. Those who decide to take a higher degree or another performance subject can also catch up on courses as block lessons. Depending on the learning type, a student can learn the same knowledge as frontal teaching, project teaching or free learning.

The solution for a peaceful and equitable learning environment on an equal footing is the import of separation of powers and its democratic control in educational institutions. Learners and teachers meet in assemblies of their course, year group and educational institution. There, rules are agreed, problems are solved and staff are elected according to the committee procedure. This represents the legislative power. The executive power is made up of learners who are assigned in turn as supervisors and helpers by an assembly. The education court is where crimes are tried in the first instance, with lawyers and judges made up of teachers and learners elected by all participants involved in a course, year group or educational institution. The mediating force is the Education Directory, where all learners, teachers, courses and assemblies are digitally stored and can be contacted, commented on and rated. Certain views and ratings remain hidden for data protection reasons.

4.8.2 Incapacitated teachers

Teachers are forced to use certain teaching methods during their training and are taught them during their traineeship. They can hardly develop their own forms and have no possibility to test successful methods and share them with all teachers. They are given their requirements as to what knowledge they have to teach and when. They have to keep records and grade how well their students know or can apply this knowledge. Written performance records are the predominant form of examination, which then have to be corrected and graded. This bureaucratic effort is unnecessary if it is not scientifically recorded in order to link appropriate learning content, teaching methods and learning types. It takes time away from lesson preparation and specialisation on individual students. In rating, teachers may give unfair marks without another teacher or students being able to effectively control it. Most teachers do not have professional experience in the subject they teach. Their teaching therefore often lacks examples and they themselves lack the ability to recognise innovations or talents.

The solution is a training of teachers that is equivalent to the study of the subject and is marked by business and school internships. Teachers are placed in different positions in the state and in companies during their professional life, so that they gain 10 years of professional experience outside educational institutions. Teachers organise themselves as colleagues in councils, which bring in projects and elect their school leadership with the learners. They may specialise in one or more forms of teaching of their election and offer their lessons on a weekly or block basis. They present their learning content at the beginning of a learning year and use it to advertise for participants in their courses. If their courses are repeatedly under-attended, their students' grade point average is too poor and the results from surveys of their students are too negative, they are transferred and dismissed the second time around. Teachers do not have to draft or correct their own performance records. The Examinations Office designs central performance records for each course each year. The correction is done by teachers from another educational institution who do not know which student's work is from.

4.8.3 Repeat class level

Having to repeat a class level, So-called "sitting", even though not all grades in all subjects are unsatisfactory, causes a loss of life and friends. In some subjects there is boredom, in others excessive demands. The solution is to give learners a choice of which courses to take and when. What level of knowledge is required in a course is made public. Courses in which one has poor grades can be pushed to the end or several teaching methods can be taken simultaneously or consecutively in several courses of the same subject. The possibility of learning a particular subject full-time is made possible by courses that are offered as block courses over several days and weeks at a time. This allows learners to determine their own educational path and set different learning speeds depending on their abilities.

4.8.4 Uncoordinated education system

The education system includes nursery schools, primary schools, various comprehensive schools, vocational schools, vocational training colleges, universities and adult education centres. All these educational institutions are not located in one ministry and are also regulated differently in all regions. Each educational institution also approaches learning differently. While it is more playful in nursery schools, timetables in schools influence the entire rhythm of life and learning. Only in some courses of study at universities is it still possible for students to freely design their own timetables. Changing education systems after a move is not possible without problems. There is no comparability of degrees, which creates disadvantages in terms of admission to jobs or colleges. School dropouts find it difficult to connect to the labour market and can only catch up on degrees at a high cost at a few educational institutions. Continuing education takes a lot of time and costs a lot of money. Transition between educational institutions and cooperation between them is inadequately regulated, haphazardly and linked to regional boundaries. This weakens the productive capacity of the entire education system.

The solution is five types of schools that complement each other and conduct research and development in education with each other. Crèches and nursery schools are combined in day care centres and exchange materials, teachers and children with primary schools. Learners determine their timetables in voting with teachers. Comprehensive schools and colleges exchange rooms, materials, teachers and support staff for tutoring, homework, sports and leisure. Learners and teachers determine their timetables themselves digitally and an algorithm in the Education Directory automatically distributes the appropriate rooms, learners and teachers according to their majority wishes. Through the nationwide central performance records and final assignments, moves become problem-free, degrees are comparable nationwide and successes of teaching methods are visible for different types of learners. Through a digitalisation of all educational content of state educational institutions in the Knowledge Directory, every lesson can also be experienced digitally and only the final examination takes place with all other examinees in one educational institution. The Knowledge Directory is also available on the Internet and serves as an extended Wikipedia with content that has been reviewed and rated by teachers.

4.8.5 Inappropriate curriculum

The curriculum does not adequately provide the knowledge to be able to do the job of an executive. Theoretical knowledge to be able to apply practically and social manners are hardly included in the curriculum during compulsory education and if so then only in different types of schools. Parents or entrepreneurs complain to teachers or school administrators about the lack of qualifications of the learners for a successful working and private life. The teachers cannot and do not have to change anything because the requirements come from the ministry and they are civil servants who have to follow the instructions from the ministry without influence.

The solution is a curriculum that is democratically negotiated, like an election manifesto for a politician's pre-election. The people can veto it if they are dissatisfied with the curriculum. The curriculum defines what skills are needed in the labour market now and in the future. Companies, state and cultural institutions are involved in teaching, through visits, internships and commissioned work by companies in educational institutions. The curriculum includes subjects that are found in all educational areas, so that research can be done in this subject area in all educational institutions involved. When learners make discoveries or inventions, they can publish or market them with the help of all educational institutions. For example, starting a business is on the curriculum in a course where a wide variety of skills are needed.

4.9 Health

The problems in health policy are manifold and also affect the environment. The bureaucratic burden keeps health workers from healing. The solution is a Health Card per person and a Health Directory in which all data from treatments are filmed and automatically entered by voice.

4.9.1 Too many unnecessary health insurance companies

Many health insurance companies spend a lot of money on boards, buildings and staff. This money is missing in health care. Patients incur most of their total costs in the last three months of their lives so they are kept alive at all costs, no matter how old they are. Some patients get sick from consuming addictive substances and others who do not consume these addictive substances have to pay for this consumption with their contributions.

The solution is three state health insurance schemes that insure general preventive care, illness and injury, and drug use or immortality. Billing and auditing are automated in the Health Directory, which records, compares and evaluates methods, costs and effects. This makes unnecessary operations and other possible cures obvious.

The problem with drugs is their potential impurity, criminal procurement and cost of medical treatment. The solution is the legalisation of all drugs, purity laws for each drug and Addictive drugs Health Insurance, the contribution to which is included in the price of the drug.

4.9.2 No health insurance approval despite healing

Only those who have successfully completed a medical degree are considered physicians, although not all healing methods are taught there. This gives the people the impression that only there they can get well. There is no freedom of choice for patients because the services of other healers are not paid for by the compulsory insurance.

The solution is to divide doctors into physicians and healers and to allow all their healing methods, which have made a minimum number of humans healthy, to be billed to the health insurance fund.

The lack of chairs, research and studies on the effectiveness of alternative healing methods promotes charlatans and prevents traditional or novel healing methods from spreading. Side effects and interactions of different healing methods, medicines and drugs can possibly do more damage to the patient than good.

The solution again lies in the digitalised healthcare system through the Health Directory and the Health Card. Through all the data of diagnosis, treatment and medication, studies are continuously run to evaluate effectiveness and costs. Patients, physicians and the research-based pharmaceutical industry gain admission to the results of the studies. Patients can obtain diagnoses and choose physicians and medicines for treatment that match the diagnoses. Physicians see which successful methods other physicians use and can also offer them to their patients. The pharmaceutical industry sees which products are cheap, effective and tolerable or cause side effects or interactions.

4.9.3 Profits from patients who remain ill

Hospitals that are part of corporations and pay dividends to shareholders are also problematic. In order to make more profits, they perform more treatments than necessary or cut corners on hygiene or staff. The solution is state and Non-profit hospitals, a medical fee schedule that covers all healing methods, and health auditors who check compliance with standards. Patients can then choose a private, state or Non-profit hospital.

The pharmaceutical industry influences physicians through training courses financed by them or free samples of medicines together with small gifts. Physicians have to attend training courses to keep their licence, and they can dispense medicines without going through a pharmacy. This costly lobbying effort pushes cures without medicines or with freely available plants out of the market. The solution is a different pharmaceutical industry in all four economic forms and a pharmaceutical industry association that publicly negotiates prices and quantities with the Ministry of Health for orders from the Health Directory. While the remedies in the Barter Economy and Planned Economy consist of free natural remedies, the pharmaceutical industry in the Social Market Economy is Non-profit and in the Free Market Economy unregulated.

4.9.4 Haphazardly through the pandemic

The healthcare system is not sufficiently prepared for a pandemic. The measures taken by governments come at short notice and change frequently. Their effectiveness is tested during implementation and faults are constantly corrected. The population becomes confused and can no longer plan their lifestyles independently.

The solution is an emergency plan for pandemics that is coordinated and practised with the population before the disaster. Adjustments to this emergency plan are then easier for the citizens to understand and an end is always foreseeable through the emergency plan. The citizens learn to assess the emergency situation and to adapt their behaviour accordingly and for a limited period of time.

4.9.5 Health-threatening environmental pollution

The problem of environmental pollution is the sometimes life-threatening effects for future generations. Environmentally protective innovations are delayed and held back by interest groups. Products often only last as long as the warranty or cause damage during production or use, the costs of which must be borne by the general public. The profits remain with the producers and are not used to cover the costs.

The solution is a cost-neutral overall concept for structural change for environmental and climate protection. Procrastination of innovation becomes a criminal offence in corporate criminal law. Products are tested for their durability and environmental safety in long-term studies before and during marketing. If they pass the first test, they receive a seal of approval. If they do not pass tests in the long-term study, they can lose the seal of approval again or have to provide information on the minimum shelf life. By the law that manufacturers have to include disposal costs in the purchase price, they agree with the disposal companies on production methods that involve as little or no disposal costs as possible. Natural degradability and a residue-free circular economy are thus promoted. The prices for waste disposal and electricity remain the same until the revenues have eliminated all the damage that has occurred so far. After that, these costs decrease because no more raw materials need to be added.

4.10 Infrastructure

The problems in infrastructure policy concern the networks, raw materials, waste, real estate, transport and energy. Supplies are in danger of being inadequate due to outdated technologies, supporting future generations. The solution is an infrastructure policy that prescribes the switch to new technologies by law and drives it forward with state funds.

4.10.1 Obsolete networks

The networks are outdated and too slow for today's demands. Renewals and repairs are not considered during construction. A nationwide water network is not available and drinking water sources are partly privatised and exploit groundwater. The solution is networks that carry all the necessary pipes in one tube and include empty pipes for retrofitting. Area-wide water pipes can pump fresh and salt water underground across the country to avert floods and droughts.

4.10.2 Exploitation of domestic raw materials

The finite natural resources in the country are exploited by joint-stock companies that distribute their profits to international shareholders and are managed by them. Future generations of the local population are deprived of the benefits. The solution is an increasing replacement of finite raw materials and their extraction under democratic control of the entire population.

4.10.3 Expensive disposal and insufficient recycling

Waste is a problem because it is widespread in the environment and its disposal is often cumbersome and expensive. Rarely can it be recycled effortlessly. Bulky waste is no longer picked up on one date in one locality and citizens cannot legally help themselves to it. Toxins from waste accumulate in the food chain and reduce natural growth.

The solution is free disposal because manufacturers must already price in these costs and transfer them to the disposal companies. Products become recyclable because manufacturers and disposers have to coordinate degradable and recyclable parts and form a circular economy. Bulky waste is put on the street on a date and is available there free of charge for citizens until it is collected by collectors from the Planned Economy and eventually the disposal companies. Collectors from Planned Economy specialise in upgrading, repairing and marketing bulky waste and e-waste.

4.10.4 Overpriced real estate market

Construction projects take a long time to be approved and yet often draw the displeasure of residents or those affected. The solution is citizen participation through debate and voting, and a state Construction Team that can implement modular construction projects at lightning speed.

Property prices are rising or are unjustifiably high. Property appraisals are difficult to find in order to be able to assess the price-performance ratio as a buyer or tenant. The solution is a Real Estate Directory in which all properties and their data on purchase price, rent and building condition are stored. As soon as the property is to be rented or sold, this data is publicly displayed.

Foreign states, companies and persons can buy land and thus drive up property prices or even take over the land. The solution is a ban on foreigners buying land.

The tenant ratio is too high and thus rising co-prices can trigger a loss of purchasing power in the population. Hundreds of thousands of state-owned flats have been sold to joint-stock companies and bring profits from rental income through dividend payments out of the country, which additionally weakens purchasing power. It is becoming increasingly difficult for domestic residents to buy housing. The state encourages rent dependency through its supposed social housing, especially for low-income citizens. The solution is state housing construction in voting with the future residents and their purchase of the housing space in a hire-purchase procedure.

4.10.5 Wasteful traffic

Obsolete traffic with internal combustion engines, abrasion and rolling noise from wheels, and roads and rails that cut up the landscape is a growing problem. The resulting costs are charged to the general public and not borne by the producers. On the contrary, only the producers bear the profits generated by transport. The charges for the transport of goods and the taxes or fees for transport are not sufficient to cover all these costs. The transport turnaround is prevented by lobbying by outdated industries and corrupt or unimaginative politicians. Transport to space generates space junk that becomes such dangerous projectiles in Earth orbit, creating a grid that turns the Earth into a prison.

The solution is a new type of transport with cars that have a battery that can be changed at filling stations or run on hydrogen or can also fly. Persons travel with it on roads or airways in autopilot or with a magnetic levitation train whose track stands on pillars. Goods are transported in underground vacuum tubes and with a suspended maglev train that runs between pillars. Ships are powered by wind, electricity or hydrogen. The Construction Team takes care of the construction of the transport routes. The transport turnaround is financed by a loan that is repaid with the levies and revenues from transport. After that, the levies, such as the CO_2 levy, tolls for freight transport, motor vehicle tax or mineral oil tax, will no longer apply. Space debris is captured by new types of space vehicles or directed into the Earth's atmosphere to burn up. Regulations on space travel will prevent space debris in the future.

4.10.6 Finite and harmful energy production

The problem with energy policy lies in the current generation, transmission and storage. Electricity, heat and fuels are generated with fossil fuels, constantly consuming raw materials that took the earth millions of years to produce. The extraction and provision of these raw materials is complex, expensive and pollutes the environment. The same applies to the disposal of the residual materials. These costs have so far been passed on to future generations and risk making the planet harder for humans to inhabit. For example, mining and the collapse of abandoned tunnels have caused So-called mine water to become contaminated with toxic minerals from the surrounding layers of the earth. As it rises, the groundwater is poisoned and can no longer be used for drinking water. Pumps transport the poisoned mine water through pipes past the groundwater and channel it into rivers and seas. This So-called eternal task pollutes the oceans and the global water cycle in the long term. Other examples are emitted CO_2 in the air, which leads to global warming, or nuclear waste, which emits life-threatening radiation for millennia. The So-called energy turnaround does not involve citizens, but allows originators to spin off their legacy waste into other companies and go bankrupt. Renewable energies generated by plants that can only be disposed of as hazardous waste generate costs for future generations.

The solution is renewable energies that do not require high technology and hazardous waste. The citizens thus support themselves decentrally and industry is supplied via central power plants at suitable locations. Power lines run underground and their waste heat is turned back into electricity through heat exchangers. On the coasts, there are marine power plants consisting of wave and tidal power plants under water and wind turbines above water. Electricity and water from estuaries is transported inland through tunnels. Pumped-storage power stations in mountains and lakes are operated with the water to store the electricity from the coast. The water can be cooled via heat exchangers and used to support district heating. Old coal-fired power plants can be converted into such heat exchangers. Old nuclear power plants can continue to run on liquid salt, which can store energy. Houses support themselves with energy and use rainwater for their pumped-storage power stations and heat exchangers, sun for heat and electricity, and wind for electricity. Excess energy is shared via transmission lines.

4.11 Security

The problems in security policy range from external to internal and private security. Both the domestic and the foreigner are affected. Only the Ministry of Security at home can contribute to the solution. Foreigner conflicts can be shielded or solved jointly by mutual agreement between several states.

4.11.1 Exploitative foreign missions

The problem with war is that it destroys infrastructure and kills, wounds or displaces humans. Today, the military hardly contributes to external security, because interstate disputes can be resolved through diplomacy. Military strength is supposed to serve as a deterrent against winning a war with heavy losses. Keeping a military strong and modern is very expensive and is called cold war because these costs weaken the economy and purchasing power of the affected taxpaying inhabitants of the opposing countries. During this cold war, armies conduct foreign missions to capture raw materials, markets and manpower in underdeveloped countries. After all, professional soldiers and modern weapon systems are supposed to pay off and old devices or ammunition are supposed to be used up before their expiry date. It is striking that highly equipped states are acting as world police and invading countries with much less well-equipped militaries. When I was doing my basic military service, I was trained for foreign missions, no longer for national defence. I learned to build and guard checkpoints, break up demonstrations by force of arms and protect targets from the angry population. I would have preferred to learn how to defend my homeland, where my family and friends live, against a foreigner's war of aggression. These acts of war with armed force abroad take place without a democratic vote by the affected peoples. For the international financial market, however, they are a lucrative business.

Refugee flows secure cheap labour or the unemployed so that wages remain low and full employment does not occur, even though the population in the industrialised nations is shrinking due to a lack of sufficient births. Unequal living conditions between domestic and refugees cause envy, fear and hatred. This divides the population to rebel against each other rather than against the responsible politicians. The costs of integrating the refugees are borne by the population. The profits from lower wages for unskilled foreigners and dividends or interest from arms corporations flow to international investors via the stock exchanges. Raw materials are exploited by corporations of the industrial nations without letting the domestic population benefit from the profits, but taxing the profits in the industrial nation and distributing them to the international shareholders. The costs of the environmental damage are charged to the local population and lead to shortages, crop failures and diseases. Sales markets are created for corporations from the industrialised nations, which squeeze out local suppliers in a price war and tax the profits in the industrialised nation and pay them out to their owners. The money from the profits is not spent in the country where they are made, thus weakening the purchasing power of the population there. Foreign missions for supposed peacekeeping have not improved the conditions of the population, but have created an expectation of dependence on great powers. Moreover, they create terrorism because humans are forced by force of arms to hand over the state's monopoly on the use of force to foreign powers. This policy state of affairs is objected to by parts of the affected population. Because the political leadership refuses to consider the interests of the affected people, parts of the affected population resign or flee and others go underground to use armed attacks as a defence. As they do not have armies of equal strength, they use guerrilla tactics and carry out So-called terrorist attacks.

My experience of this comes from a visit to NATO and SHAPE in Brussels. There I learned how the Taliban came into being, namely through the arbitrary drawing of borders by the former colonial power and the United Nations through the territory of the Taliban, without involving them in the shaping of the border. I learned how profit is made from war from a conversation with an analyst at the German stock exchange in Frankfurt. He explained to me the global view of international investors.

The solution is to end all foreign missions and create a defence-only army. To keep costs as low as possible, barracks, devices and soldiers are used for social security in peacetime. The military is organised on the militia principle, so that the population receives military training, converts to a war economy in the event of defence, and participates in combat operations. In peacetime, they all pursue their private gainful and leisure activities. As soon as several neighbouring countries unify in an alliance, they can defend their common external borders with less effort, divide up tasks and save costs. Investors are given the opportunity to profit from the upswing in countries that still need to catch up with the highest currently possible standard of living.

4.11.2 Destructive arms industry

Weapons have the problem of only being able to destroy things, which causes costs. They offer no added value. They can provide security when used by democratically controlled security forces. Currently, however, weapons are misused to exercise power. The arms industry is enriched by conditions in which undemocratic rulers force their populations to obey and exploit them. The profits of the arms industry flow as taxes to the states that host them and to the investors who hold their company shares or debts. This misuse of weapons fosters a circuit of violence and constantly creates more demand for weapons and contaminates generations with psychological suffering.

The solution is to produce weapons in companies that only switch their production when needed and produce as many weapons as are required by the security forces. The export of weapons or production facilities for weapons is banned.

4.11.3 Disproportionate arming of the security forces

Lethal weapons used by security forces against their own population have the disadvantage that they are rarely used and have therefore lost their deterrent effect. On the contrary, they pose a risk of being stolen. Their use against persons who do not have similar weapons is disproportionate and tends to lead to extrajudicial punitive measures.

The solution is to use non-lethal weapons, which are deployed more quickly. Lethal weapons are only used by special task forces to fight attackers armed with lethal weapons.

4.11.4 Political abuse of the powerless police force

The problem with the police is that they have too little time for law enforcement and their painstaking work is undone by court judgments. inland, the police are increasingly disrespected because politicians too often use them to prevent citizens from protesting against political grievances. When I saw the mass of police at demonstrations, encircling demonstrators or separating them from counter-demonstrators, I felt sorry for the police. When I talked to policemen about my condition, they said they are not allowed to talk about politics with demonstrators, not allowed to show solidarity, even though they feel the same as nationals. When they have to search for and seize criminals again and again because they are acquitted, only briefly detained or not deported, it weakens their morale. If they are then insulted, spat on or fought, hatred builds up. There are neighbourhoods where the police no longer dare to go, or only with considerable manpower. In addition, there are punitive measures and criminal prosecution for offences that do not endanger any humans, but are nevertheless forbidden. Examples of this are the illegality of drugs and fights or the tabooing of love and sexuality in the law. The bureaucratic effort to log all these unnecessary criminalisations ties up additional working time for the prosecution of trained professionals.

The solution is a police force that operates nationwide and cooperates with police forces in neighbouring states. It is supported in patrol duty by a state security service called People's Protection Service, which also provides emergency social services. The police focus on solving violent crimes and theft. The People's Protection Service consists of one police officer per patrol, soldiers on community service, People's Service providers and volunteers. Cities that exceed a crime rate of 10,000 crimes per year per 100,000 inhabitants are completely searched during a city raid. Demonstrations are accompanied by People's Motor Vehicles to voice the opinion of the demonstrators and find solutions. Criminal foreigners are deported after serving their sentence and banned from entering the country for life. Police officers wear a body camera that documents everything and replaces the protocols. Police officers are allowed to use light force immediately if they are offended and to use non-lethal weapons in case of any danger to themselves or involuntaries. If all those affected agree to violence being inflicted on them, police merely secure bystanders. The People's Protection Service organises brawls and collects fees for Addictive drugs Health Insurance from the participants involved. Drugs are legal and include a fee for Addictive drugs Health Insurance. Love and sex is legalised by the Registry Office's certification of voluntary.

4.11.5 Secret services in action against their own people

The problem with secret services is their secret espionage operations against their own population and allies. In general, secret actions of the state pose the danger of acting against the will of the people because they cannot be democratically controlled. As soon as a politician has to spy on his own people, there is a political fault that makes this necessary.
The solution is a civilian police force that secretly investigates all criminals and brings them before a responsible court. The foreign secret services and military secret services of all participating member states of the European Union will be merged as soon as possible into the European secret service. Its head will be directly elected.

4.11.6 Private security services without democratic control

The problem with private security services is that the monopoly on the use of force no longer resides exclusively with the state and is thus democratically controlled. Thousands of workers with training in the use of force under the leadership of a private or foreigner company pose a threat to public security and order.

The solution is the state security service called People's Protection Service. Citizens can order it for their neighbourhood in case of a majority feeling of insecurity, companies can do it for their buildings and premises.

4.11.7 Borderless crime and economic flight

The problem with border management is the insufficient information about persons, goods, services and capital between states. While money and many goods can easily cross borders, this is not the case for persons. The current customs policy is unable to redress the imbalance. This imbalance leads to illegal immigration, cross-border theft and trade in illegal goods, and tax evasion. This problem becomes particularly severe when borders are opened but law enforcement, immigration policy and trade policy are not uniformly regulated and jointly organised in all participating countries. The Schengen area is an example of how inadequate border protection leads to cross-border burglary.

The solution is to return to blanket border controls in the short term until there is a European police force, immigration is managed on the basis of quotas of foreign nationals, and all requirements for trade in goods and services are standardised. The European Union's external borders will be sealed off until a uniform standard of living is achieved within all peoples of the member states. Remaining foreign trade is managed with tariffs, which prevent exploitation through price differences due to different living standards. Immigration is managed with visas. They are temporary and can only become permanent through naturalisation. Whether naturalisation is possible is decided by the municipal and national quota of foreigners.

4.11.8 Haphazardly disaster management

The problem with disaster management is that it is uncoordinated and short-tempered. The country is repeatedly hit by similar natural disasters, but the population never knows what will happen to them. Those affected live in uncertainty and existential fear during or after a disaster. During reconstruction, the state relief workers do not stay until the original situation is restored, but leave beforehand. Affected people have to wait a long time for craftspersons because all businesses in the affected region are fully booked. The costs and the waiting time increase.

When I helped flood victims in 2013 for a week three weeks after the disaster, there were only volunteers left on the ground and there was still so much to do. Those affected reported the above conditions to me.

The solution consists of emergency plans that are already coordinated and practised with the population before a disaster. Everyone is given a specific task as a private emergency worker in a particular disaster. Through an early warning system, all state and private emergency forces as well as the affected population in the disaster area are alerted by signals from sirens. Voluntary helpers are transported to the disaster area free of charge by public transport, affected people are evacuated, trades and construction companies are organised nationwide and all available security forces are deployed for transport, supply, food and repair. The mission will not end until reconstruction is complete.

4.12 Justice

The problems with justice lie with judges, court proceedings, punitive measures and criminal law. The solution is democratisation and simplification of procedures.

4.12.1 Partisan judges

Judges pronounce judgements in the name of the people, but are only indirectly bound to the will of the people, namely through laws enacted by elected representatives. For plaintiffs and defendants, it is a matter of luck which judge they end up with, how he applies the laws and how well he gets along with the respective lawyer. Because judges are tenured, they can easily maintain this favouritism.

The solution is directly elected judges who are deselected if there is sufficient dissatisfaction among the population about their rulings.

4.12.2 Unaffordable lengthy court proceedings

Court proceedings usually take a long time and cost a lot of money. The courts are overloaded with cases, which creates a long waiting time. Sometimes the costs are so high that injured parties shy away from court proceedings because they cannot pay for them. The duration is sometimes so long that the causes of the proceedings or the ordered standstill already have damaging effects. The long duration of proceedings sometimes drives plaintiffs or defendants to financial ruin, which is caused by the overburdening of the courts or the wealth of the opposing side and the course through all instances. Long periods between the offence and the verdict prevent the learning effect in offenders that can re-socialise them.

The solution is court proceedings with digitised files containing police investigations and lawyers' letters as text, sound or video in order to be able to present facts in a virtual simulation. In addition, the arbitration procedure creates a digital instance before the first instance. It can be used on a voluntary basis or is obligatory for cases with a value in dispute of less than 1000 euros and without relevance to society as a whole. Court proceedings are initially financed by the Ministry of Justice and at the end of the proceedings the losers bear the costs. The costs amount to cost-covering fees and 10% profits. This allows capacities to be expanded or reduced in order to always have sufficient rooms and staff. In sentence and constitutional law, the costs of proceedings are financed by value added tax. The more effectively the laws are formulated and the more peaceable and civilly courageous the population is, the lower the costs.

4.12.3 Expensive penal system

Suspended sentences are an administrative burden and prevent offenders from learning. The solution is no longer to impose suspended sentences, but directly community service or detention. This makes compensation possible and revenues that cover the costs of the penal system.

Detention currently costs more money than is developed by the prisoners. Prisoners also receive money from their work in detention and can sometimes afford more than citizens in freedom. The solution is detention with the most valuable work possible, performed by prisoners with the appropriate skills. The wages go to the victims as compensation and to the state as reparations to society for its impaired sense of security.

4.12.4 Unclear legal situations

Criminal law is currently issued by the Ministry of Justice. Therefore, violations of laws of other ministries are not punished or not punished effectively because the legislators come from different ministries. The solution is criminal law enacted by the responsible ministries. The Ministry of Justice is only involved in this to ensure interpretation in the spirit of the drafters.

Incomprehensible, complicated or outdated laws are also problematic. The population cannot understand the meaning of laws and therefore finds it difficult to comply with them. Laws with which the population is dissatisfied cannot be changed by them. Moreover, the jurisprudence finds it difficult to interpret the laws and justify its verdict to the convicted. The solution is a Law Directory in which all norms are listed and can be amended or abolished by means of a repeal quorum. Norms are all rules from international law, European law, constitutional articles, laws, court judgments, regulations and so on. All norms are filmed and broadcast as a video before they are voted on.

4.13 Foreign Affairs

The problem with foreign policy is that international anarchy prevents world peace and neoliberal globalisation causes exploitation. The solution is an international policy that only becomes effective when all affected peoples have agreed.

4.13.1 International anarchy

Every foreign policy has to contend with the fact that anarchy prevails internationally, which prevents world peace. This means that sovereign states can make agreements, but if they are not respected there is no police or justice that can punish this. An action by another state can only be completely influenced by war. There is no monopoly on the use of force to punish worldwide crimes according to the laws of the rule of law with prosecution and jurisprudence. As in ancient times, the law of the strongest applies. The unification of states into federal states, So-called federalism, reduces the number of states and can also shift the balance of power through its new size. In most cases, unifications of states have been accompanied by revolutionary struggles and enforced by force. Sometimes old rulers have been overthrown, sometimes new rulers have come to power. In the past, there were aristocrats, later dictators on the political left or right, who extended the sphere of influence of their power through war. Today, there are undemocratic international organisations, such as the United Nations, the United Nations, NATO or free trade agreements, as well as internationally trading rentiers who make investments without democratic morals in order to make money with money. Because there is no global state, criminals can do damage in one country and settle in another country where they will not be prosecuted. Today, however, only those who have a lot of money can travel and settle without borders. The law of the rich applies. The rich, who own companies and government bonds that span the globe, are able to assert their power against any national monopoly on the use of force. They control the supply of money and goods. Politicians are their fulfilment agents because they are their debtors.

The solution is a clear regularisation of the communitarisation of states and an equally clear demarcation against international markets through Self-sufficiency of the citizens and the whole country. Only when countries are able to support themselves can they unify independently. A partnership formed out of dependency always carries risks and discord. This is why there are rings of integration that states go through on the way to unification. While only common laws and agencies emerge at first, common ministers, ministries and parties follow later. Finally, communitarisation ends with a common constitution in which peoples unite to form a nation. This process is first run-through by states that are geographically and culturally close to each other. These So-called united states of the continents then newly start the same process until there are only the united states of the world.

In the short term, countries close themselves off to learn how to support themselves without depending on other countries. In the medium term, they open up to their neighbouring countries and unify with culturally similar peoples on their continent. In the long term, there are no more foreigners. Races and minorities survive in cultural protection areas, cosmopolitans live around them with slight municipal differences and a common constitution applies to all humans. A common monopoly on the use of force is responsible for all, because only the ministries of security and justice may not be administered municipally. The European Union is an example of how states can communitarise peacefully, avoid war on their continent and still benefit from economies of scale in the international market. European Union policies are democratised and the exploitation of poorer member states by richer member states is stopped, making living standards the same across Europe. Other countries on other continents follow suit and adapt their policies to each other rather than forcing them to follow European policies. The more countries adopt this system, the easier international action becomes because the systems are all the same. This makes it clear to everyone who is responsible for what in a country, because the ministries and their offices are all called the same. When all the states of the world are finally unified in a federal state, there will be no need for an army or a Ministry of Foreign Affairs. The military is only necessary to defend humanity against celestial bodies or hostile aliens.

4.13.2 Exploitative globalisation

The problem with globalisation is its historically grown exploitative character, which does more damage than good to a majority of domestic citizens and foreigners. Globalisation began in the age of imperialism with colonies, abduction, human trafficking, forced labour and the exploitation of raw materials, and still shapes international migration movements today. Today, humans are fleeing from war zones and impoverished states to the industrialised nations that once laid the foundation for the crises in these countries. An example of this are refugees from Afghanistan, where borders were arbitrarily drawn through tribal areas after colonial times, tribes became enemies and were repeatedly prevented from regional demarcation by occupying forces. Today, a neoliberal global market economy circuit is at work, trading humans, money, companies, goods and services around the world and distributing the profits to a rich few.

Global economic migration of persons, goods, services and capital generates high profits from the different living standards of the populations between the countries where companies produce or sell. This business model creates an incentive for joint-stock company investors to continue to provide different standards of living around the world. Investors can strategically invest money to affect the prices of food, fuel and currencies differently in different countries. Through government bonds issued by indebted states, investors gain direct influence over politicians because, as creditors, they can use their interest to drive up state budget costs or even trigger a state bankruptcy. Through this mechanism, a worldwide ruinous circular economy is set in motion.

The solution is to renounce international border demarcation and interference in the internal affairs of a foreigner without its consent, as well as no deployment of military forces or arms supplies. Weapons do not create peace, democratic structures do, with which solutions are found together and responsible politicians are elected. For example, in Afghanistan, ethnic groups can organise themselves into municipalities and alliances of municipalities, administer themselves in certain ministries and define nationwide responsibilities in nationally administered ministries. Tariffs, visas and import or export bans prevent the exploitation of differences in living standards between states. Tariffs can bring production prices or sales prices up to the level of the Country-of-destination, thus equalising living standards. Visas can regulate and limit the stay of foreigners in the country. Import bans can prevent the influence of foreign companies or investors. Export bans on state-subsidised goods prevent dumping prices. For example, an export ban on state-subsidised goods can have the effect of creating a dairy industry in North Africa because there is no longer any European milk powder that is cheaper than locally produced milk could ever be. Guest work is now only possible in the Free Market Economy and in the Social Market Economy only in exceptional cases. World trade without regularisation is only allowed in the Free Market Economy. Other economic forms are cut off from it by restrictions and their own currencies. The company founders, investors, employees and customers can decide which economic form they want to participate in. As soon as other states have also established a Barter Economy or Planned Economy, trade can also be conducted between these economic forms.

4.13.3 Ineffective development aid

The problem with development aid is that it has been around for a long time and in that time it has failed to raise the standard of living in a third world country, So-called developing countries, to that of a first world country, So-called developed countries. Current development aid alleviates the need, but not the cause of the need. Aid supplies of food and consumer goods are consumed by the needy and then they are again dependent on aid. For example, noodles and oil are given to starving people. Aid is purchased in the donor country by the donor country providing development aid and delivered to the developing country. This means that the profits from the value added during production remain in the donor country. For example, a truck from Daimler is delivered to Congo as development aid. The jobs and tax revenues are not created in the developing country. Branches in developing countries of companies from industrialised nations make profits in the developing country and broadcast them to their country of origin. The affected population is held captive and exploited. Development aid is haphazardly and uncoordinated. Many honorary, Non-profit or state aid organisations pursue different purposes and do not consult with each other or the affected people when distributing their funds. Funds are distributed drop by drop on hot stones. Many developing countries receive little money per developing country over a long period of time.

The solution is to help people to help themselves, to educate the affected population about the overall plan and to involve many individual residents in a targeted way at different points in the plan. In order to have sufficient personnel, material and money, all development aid is concentrated on only one developing country until it is developed to the point where the population can support itself on its own. After that, the development workers move on to the next neighbouring developing country. Different continents sponsor each other. For example, North America provides development aid in South America and Europe in Africa. As soon as there are no more developing countries and the same standard of living prevails worldwide, development aid is discontinued.

4.14 Integration

The problem with integration lies in the poor legal and democratic design of citizenship, naturalisation, integration, immigration and asylum. Exceeding the speed of integration overburdens domestic people to accept newcomers into their community. For example, a new child is accepted into a class more quickly than if there are five who also know each other. The solution is to measure the speed of integration through surveys and voting. Citizens are asked what percentage of foreigners they want in the overall population and in their locality, and whether immigrants should adapt, i.e. assimilate, or whether the two groups should adapt to each other, i.e. integrate. Immigrants are asked whether they want to stay or return to their country of origin and whether they prefer to integrate or assimilate. The Integration Directory is used for distribution.

4.14.1 Discriminatory dual citizenship

The problem with citizenship is the possibility of having several nationals. This favours humans with multiple nationals because they live in multiple states and have a democratic say. They are not so dependent on the health of the country, its people and future generations. For example, German Turks can live and vote in Germany and in Turkey. They can live according to conservative Muslim values in Germany and support such a government in both countries. At the same time, they are neither recognised by Germans as Germans, nor by Turks as Turks. They can hardly become at home in one country.

The solution is to prohibit the possession of one or more other nationalities in addition to the domestic citizenship. If necessary, domestic citizenship is withdrawn. Domestic citizenship can arise through love and sex if a child is conceived by domestic parents. If a child has parents with both domestic and foreign nationals, he or she may choose domestic or foreign nationality until the age of majority.

4.14.2 Parallel societies

The problem with naturalisation is that it promotes coexistence rather than togetherness. The construction of neighbourhoods with many small rented flats and the mass settlement of foreigners promotes ghettoisation, exclusion and crime. For example, in some places it is possible to live inland without being able to speak the national language, but only a foreign language. In the social environment of children growing up there are no nationals in the family, among friends, neighbours or colleagues. Moreover, the children are given foreign names. Naturalisation becomes almost impossible under all these circumstances.

The solution is different requirements that foreigners must fulfil when staying inland. While tourists and guests only receive temporary residence permits, naturalised foreigners can stay indefinitely. Naturalisation is connected with classes, examinations and certificates. Knowledge of the language and the law are thus proven, as well as a social environment with domestic friends and honorary service in clubs and rescue services.

4.14.3 Exclusion or preference of cultures and religions

The problem with integration is that some subcultures, minorities and faiths are excluded and others are favoured. For example, the sexual sado-masochism subculture and the Salafist faith are excluded and lesbians and Buddhists tend to be favoured. The solution is for radical minorities are able to segregate themselves in cultural protection areas if they are offended by the way of life of the rest of society or vice versa. Religions are separated from the state and must abide by existing laws in order not to be banned.

4.14.4 Immigration to the detriment of employees and immigrants

The problem with immigration is that it is not done out of charity, but because it is meant to prevent full employment. Employers have power over employees when there is unemployment because they can reject applicants with high standards and hire those with lower standards. This power relationship only exists when there is unemployment. When there is full employment or a labour shortage, this power relation is reversed. Employees can then influence wages and working conditions by working elsewhere and the company no longer has enough workers. Full employment occurs automatically when the birth rate is below 2 children per woman because the population shrinks.

In order for unemployment to continue, a decreasing population is prevented by immigration. Immigrants play a role in this because they should preferably be male, young, poor, uneducated, culturally diverse and traumatised, and their educational qualifications should not be internationally recognised. Men cannot escape the labour market through pregnancy and childbirth. Young humans are available to the labour market for a long time. Poor people cannot open their own companies or buy housing. Uneducated people cannot hold influential jobs. Culturally diverse humans are less likely to form alliances with domestic colleagues. Traumatised people put up with unfair working conditions. Those whose educational qualifications are not recognised cannot demand jobs or wages that match their educational qualifications. Such immigrants leave their homeland out of necessity and do not immigrate out of love for the country and its people. This fundamentally prejudices future integration. Today's refugee policy is pretty much in line with this pattern and has nothing to do with charity. It is a profit-oriented industry in which governments and international corporations earn well. Governments receive more tax revenue from increasing populations because sales increase. The standard of living, on the other hand, does not change or declines because immigrants are poorer and less educated than the domestic population. Only with integration help from the domestic population are immigrants brought up to the standard of living. The companies do not bear these costs, but they profit in wage negotiations with labour unions from the high unemployment rate and in job negotiations with applicants from their ignorance of their labour rights. Immigrants educate each other about their social rights and are supported by aid organisations in doing so. They receive social benefits and develop an attitude of entitlement without them and their parents' generations having paid in enough to build up the welfare state. Because employees pay social security contributions, employers are not affected by the costs. They profit from unemployment and employees pay the costs of the unemployed through their payroll deductions for social security and payroll taxes. The more war-torn a region is, the more aggressive and traumatised its immigrants are. Psychological care is not available to the same extent and is expensive. The domestic and foreigner populations find it more difficult to come together and are more likely to develop parallel societies and civil war-like conditions.

The solution is a quota of foreigners, in which the locals determine how and with how many immigrants they can and want to deal. Different proportions of foreigners may be possible in each municipality. However, the total number of foreigners nationwide must not be exceeded. Otherwise, residences are limited or not approved. Foreigners take part in surveys that indicate how long a foreigner intends to stay and whether he or she prefers to adapt or bring in his or her culture. By analysing and publishing the results, foreigners know where they are welcome with their attitude. Entry fees into certain economic forms and insurances enable fair participation in the costs of the social security system. Integration measures enable all immigrants to be quickly accepted into the social life of a municipality. Foreigners who need social benefits without being insured must leave the country within the time limit or are deported after the time limit has expired. Criminal foreigners are deported after serving their imprisonment and banned from entering the country for life.

4.14.5 Intolerable asylum procedures

The problem with the asylum procedure is that asylum applicants do not know whether they will be granted asylum. The hope for a better life leads them through an odyssey until they can finally file their asylum application to know for sure whether they will be granted asylum. In asylum centres, they are accustomed to inactivity, regulated by others and cared for by others. They send money to their home countries and thus also accustom the local population to being provided for by others. In addition, this causes a loss of domestic purchasing power. The fact that asylum status ends as soon as the country of origin is safe again creates a situation that tends to damage long-term ties. The hope of a right to stay is there, but the certainty is only there when the asylum status ends and the decision is made by authorities. Asylum centres are built without the consent of the local population and are sealed off from the rest of the neighbourhood.

The solution is the asylum application in embassies, the first stay in asylum houses of the Social Villages, where the asylum seekers get to know the Planned Economy and decide whether they want to be naturalised with domestic host families or prepared in Asylum Villages for the reconstruction of their country of origin. Asylum Villages are suburbs or neighbourhoods built by asylum seekers, occupied for a short time and sold for some profits. The asylum seekers do not need money inland because they live in Planned Economy or with a host family. Their assets are invested in the construction of houses in the Asylum Villages and paid out to them along with a share of the profits upon departure or naturalisation. The asylum seekers are richer after their return than before and know how a municipality can support itself.

4.15 Family

The problems with family policy concern children, parents, parenting, marriage, love and sex. Family life is unnecessarily criminalised by a lack of or inadequate rights and obligations. Aging parents with fewer children pose a problem for continued existence and economic strength. The solution is a family policy that offers rules and services in all circumstances that enable humans to grow old and reproduce in peace. Thanks to registry and Youth Welfare Offices, educational institutions, children's homes and youth centres, the age of parents becomes irrelevant and the succession of generations varies in length. As a result, population development is more stable and with fewer fluctuations in young and old humans.

4.15.1 Rightless childhood

Children's rights are insufficiently regulated. For example, it is not regulated what the best interests of the child are, although there is a criminal law for child welfare endangerment. The solution is a law on the best interests of the child, about which parents are educated in the parenting licence.

Children are not covered unconditionally, so they can survive without parents. The solution is a child benefit that is sufficient for round-the-clock care. Youth centres and children's homes in the Social Villages offer full-time care, other care services are paid for via the child benefit card.

4.15.2 Neglected youths

Youths are politically neglected. Playgrounds are forbidden for them because they exceed the age limit. Legal places to stay outside the parental home are mostly scarce. Young parents are often still dependent on their parents or overburdened.

The solution is a clan for young parents, consisting of youth centres in residential houses with social workers as permanent house residents and youths who temporarily live there and can look after each other and children of young parents. Youth centre branches are places to stay, such as tree houses or construction trailers. The Youth Alliance organises youth fire brigade and scout events throughout the country.

4.15.3 Criminalisation of love

The regulations for marriage and partnering are outdated and partly criminalise love and sex. Divorces cause cost and suffering through court proceedings, especially when children are involved. Marriage as a relationship of one man and one woman to procreate children causes unnecessary policy tailoring of love relationships. Partnering through love and sex is not regulated, which promotes uncertainties, misunderstandings and crimes.

The solution is a model for a binding marriage contract, which the spouses can amend as they wish by mutual consent, but which must agree on certain conditions after a divorce. The Registry Office certifies concluded marriage contracts and mutual consent for love or sexual relations between any number of humans of any gender.

4.15.4 Lonely senior citizens

Senior citizens are insufficiently involved in social life and easily become lonely. If they need care, their partners and friends are quickly overwhelmed. The solution is to network senior citizens in the Seniors' Alliance with Non-profit and tourist events as well as retirement homes that residents run cooperatively and let voluntary caregivers live in them rent-free.

4.15.5 Compulsion to live

Suicide is illegal and so is helping people to commit it. Conversely, this means a compulsion to live. However, life belongs to the living being itself and to no one else. The solution is to legalise suicide with a procedure that protects the bereaved and provides advice for suicides and allows them to die painlessly.

5 About the author

In this chapter I would like to write in the first person, because it is about a part of my privacy. This openness seems necessary to me because I demand trust from you, dear reader. I owe it to you to reveal my innermost thoughts so that you know whom you can or want to trust. I ask you not to use my openness against me to my disadvantage. Please always remember that you did not have to be so open with me. I don't know your journal entries, your beliefs or your resume. I am revealing this of myself because I hope you will then understand me better. I wish you to be happier in humanity. My political attitudes may not match your ideas. They don't have to be. I believe that if everyone is open about their policies, it will be easier to find solutions that suit everyone. In this chapter there are parts that I wrote in my idea diary years ago and reproduce here almost unchanged. I mark the relevant sections in *italics*.

5.1 My motivation

I am writing my book because I would like to offer all revolutions and motivated opposition politicians in the world a wealth of solutions and a complete coordinated democratic political system. I would be happy if I could still experience how my new system is made to work somewhere in the world. I am happy to help with that if the population wants me. This has always motivated me to motivate tired humans myself. I have imagined how the people are encouraged, how the mass of people rise up and become proud of themselves when they find solutions together and move the country forward at full steam. I have connected this full steam ahead with economic strength, which is used to raise living standards and reduce environmental pollution. *We humans find the second Earth because we have to, not because we have used up our home planet. We must never allow ourselves to make our mother planet uninhabitable for humans. We humans reproduce through love, so the population will grow and need more and more space.* I was happy when I found the right solutions for this. And it is precisely this joy that I can also generate in other humans by writing all these lines that has spurred me on. I want to make the heart of humanity beat faster.

5.2 My vision

My vision is to turn humanity into a being with consciousness. Politics takes over the tasks of the brain's circuitry. I was born at a time when humanity had learned to speak and could already walk. The worldwide movement of persons, products and assets has already brought damage and benefit to ongoing humanity. In my travels around the world I could observe this. The computer is the mouth of humanity. I am grateful to be able to witness how masses of people can work together today, independent of time and space. I want to make use of this possibility so that all the cells of the body of humanity can talk to each other. As different as the human races are the cells for different organs, as different as the nations are the cells in different parts of the body, as different as the tasks of a single cell are the ways of life of the people. The People's Computer is the interface of each cell to the nervous system. The intranet of People's Computers, lines, servers, operating systems and programmes is the nervous system. The media are the sense organs. Political contents are sensory impressions and reactions to them. Political processes are reaction patterns and action sequences in the various regions of the brain and parts of the body. Political structures are supply processes between the cells and organs and their flow charts in the cerebellum. My hope is to have invented an information system through the digitalised dynamic media democracy with which humanity can successfully learn to speak.

5.3 My goal

My goal is to establish a reign that is as legitimate as possible. Whether I will rule or other humans will rule based on my proposals, it is crucial to become aware of what legitimate reign means. In my political science studies, I came across Max

Weber's three forms of legitimate reign.[1] This made it clear to me what has to be given so that humans want to do what I say. Only in this way am I able to design a policy system that can have sufficient appeal.

The reign by virtue of charisma is given when people find that I am a horny guy. They follow me as long as I have a charisma that they find attractive and that gives them pleasure. I would like to claim that it never gets boring with me and that there is also at least one hearty laugh. "Jack of all trades" is a saying that describes quite well my personality of a lively, go-getting, over-zealous and nice person. I tend to be quiet and thoughtful when alone or in intimate togetherness. For me, honesty is the key to an authentic charisma. That's where I get my loose mouth from time to time. I prefer it when humans tell me honestly to my face what they think, rather than white lies or blasphemies. Every human starts with 100%. Anyone who disappoints me receives less trust from me and sinks in my favour. Whoever damages me, I avoid. If I cannot avoid him because a condition keeps imposing itself on me, I change the condition. After I have understood the cause and effect of the condition, I develop suitable ideas and test them until I am successful.

The reign by statute is given when people like what I have written. They follow me as long as I keep to it. I have written my book as detailed and understandable as possible. I have partly written things against my personal opinion that I don't like but are necessary so that people who are not like me also feel comfortable in my new system. I did not want to make the same fault as Marx or Hitler and give hate speech in my book or make unclear statements about my intentions. On the contrary, the intention was only to point out paths to be followed so that the future prospects for humanity would improve. No matter how well I would be doing in my new system, this happiness would always be in danger as long as there are humans who are worse off because of my new system.

The reign by virtue of privilege is given when people believe me to

---

1 Weber in: *Winckelmann, Johannes F.* 1952: Legitimacy and Legality in Max Weber's Sociology of Rule. With an appendix: Max Weber, The Three Pure Types of Legitimate Reign., Tübingen, p.120

come from a family of physicians through whom I developed the desire to become a physician for humanity. They follow me only as long as they believe that I have accumulated sufficient knowledge through my curriculum vitae and have linked it logically. Admittedly, it is a privilege to have grown up in a family of doctors because I have never been ill for long or seriously and have come to know the human body well. But more crucial is probably the privilege of experiencing the medical ethics of helping all humans, healing them and not doing them any damage. What is not a privilege is the constant issues of illness and accidents of various patients in the family routine. It would have been easy to become a hypochondriac there. I didn't become a physician myself because I find it hard to bear seeing how syringes or scalpels penetrate the human body. Doing that on a daily basis was out of the question for me. Politics piqued my interest because it allows you to be a physician for humanity. I think that's where the many analogies between the human body and the political organisation of humanity come from.

5.4 My beliefs

The most important sense is cheerfulness.
Things always turn out differently than you think.
Intelligent is doing what you can to achieve what you want.
Nothing ventured, nothing gained.
If not now, when? If not us, who else?
Good ideas come from God, bad ideas come from hell.
Only those who think badly are bad.
At the end of the day, it's what you leave behind in the world that counts.
The last shirt has no pockets.
In modesty one finds the happiness of having.
Clothes make the man and borders make the country, but humans always remain humans.
Helping is easy for the strong, so he can do it.
I do not forbid anything good just because there is evil.
I cannot change the past, but I can have a say in the future.
You have to know your enemies in order to be able to fight

them.

You have to know the worst in humans in order to make the best of them.

Guilt is always borne by a person or a generation. The inheritance of guilt is inadmissible.

Germany is my fatherland, the world is my native soil and the environment is my homeland.

Globalisation is near.

Respect humans who ask you, despise humans who use you, honour humans who make you happy, avoid humans who harass you.

You don't get freedom as a gift, you take it.

5.5 My educational background

I carefully collected, expanded, reconsidered all my ideas over the years, trained myself appropriately, continued my education and acquired qualification degrees. I pursued my plan single-mindedly, punctually, persistently and thoroughly in order to implement my ideas. The German virtues have served me as much as the German political and civil society system in which I grew up, as well as my family, which has given me every opportunity. My family lineage has been thoroughly German in the recent past. I have educated myself about the recent German past to the best of my knowledge and belief in order to form my consciousness of being a German national through academic and personal experiences.

My educational path was long and arduous, because it was not easy for me to write good grades until I got to university. I did reading, writing and arithmetic only for school and not in my free time. My experiences of the reality of the political system were often frightening and sobering. They also cost me a lot of time and money. I can understand that humans reject such questioning. It opens a Pandora's box of dissatisfaction. You realise where you are being cheated or exploited, when and by whom, without being able to defend yourself against it. If you don't have the hope, as I do, that you can change everything for the better with solutions, you become disaffected with politics, depressed or ready to use violence.

5.5.1 Youth

I was born in 1984 into a family with a middle-class level of education and assets. I attended a church and a municipal nursery school. Due to the divorce of my parents at the age of eight, the move from Hesse to Baden-Württemberg and back, I attended two primary schools and two grammar schools. In my college entrance qualification, French and biology were my performance subjects, history and art my other two examination subjects. I had the idea for this book at the age of 18, and from then on I geared my educational experiences to it. At 17, I was disgusted with politics and wanted to try to change something about politics instead of just complaining about it. When I joined a youth party, I quickly learned that I wouldn't get far there with ideas. Rope systems, delegate systems and list positions for offices with responsibility for government create a web of power through influence based on favour, not content, where the best idea wins out. Those who most ruthlessly exploit the faults of others and fulfil votes of party friends through bribery get to the top list positions. I did not want to go down this path because I was sure that at the end of it I would no longer be who I once was. The alternative was to found a party myself, with all my ideas for policy improvement as a party programme and a statute that would give party members with the best ideas and qualifications the top list positions until this system of list voting is replaced by a new fairer procedure.

5.5.2 Military service

As a citizen subject to compulsory military service, I decided to do basic military service with the air force after my college entrance qualification. I wanted to get an insight behind the barracks walls so as not to have a blind spot in the state. I chose the air force because, in case of doubt, I wanted to become a pilot. I ended up in the air defence in the motor pool and had to transport letter post between barracks, which could also have been sent by post. I was trained for foreign missions and learned how to keep angry demonstrators in check. Actually,

I wanted to learn how to carry out national defence by force of arms in the event of an attack on my fatherland. I had to dismantle barracks and see how national property was sold at prices far below its value. I was so mentally underchallenged that I wanted to study afterwards, even though I was fed up with learning before that.

5.5.3 Academic studies

Originally, I wanted to be a journalist, but because of my A-levels of 3.0, I applied for political science and was accepted in the backlog procedure in the state university in Frankfurt am Main. I wanted to become a journalist to get insights into all areas of politics and to get in front of the camera, so a lot of people know me and buy the book. Political science also lent itself to learning about the political spheres. I wanted to learn what a head of state needs to know to do his job as well as possible. That meant knowing the policy system as well as possible. The focus on government and policy management is not very popular among students, but for me it was the most necessary. My good fortune was that students were allowed to choose three other minor subjects for themselves, from any subject area across the university. Therefore, I attended many different lectures and seminars at different subject areas. I found law interesting and also did a certificate in public law, but as I preferred to make law rather than learn it by heart, I decided against it. Philosophy, biology, physics and art education were also courses I attended. In the end, I chose social psychology, economics and human geography. Social psychology is the psychology from two persons to masses of people. In order to manage a people in its own way, these insights were helpful. Economics is the interaction of markets for goods, services, labour, money and foreign trade. To be able to coordinate a Central Bank, economy and labour policy for the benefit of the people, I learned the necessary theory. My special luck was the chair of planned economy, where I gained insights into this past economic form. Human geography deals with urban planning and migration. I learned the necessary background knowledge there to be able to promote housing, infrastructure and integration in the future.

At the end of my studies, I wanted to check the preconceptions about Sweden that I had gathered during my studies. Sweden was often considered a prime example of how a welfare state and harmonious coexistence can succeed. Through an Erasmus scholarship, I went to the university in Linköping for one semester. There I had to put aside many good prejudices and acknowledge that I did not want to emigrate there. I knew Swedish, but Swedes shunned me when they found out I was a foreigner. I lived in the foreigners' district and attended seminars for foreign students. Getting in touch with Swedes was very difficult. Making Swedish friends was impossible. The curfews and the taboo handling of alcohol and drugs seemed strange to me. The healthcare system gave me a scarred meniscus and a crooked finger after two accidents that were not treated properly. In a weekly video diary I recorded my experiences, which were often very beautiful. So I learned to appreciate that other countries mean other manners and other systems.

5.5.4 Field studies

In my studies, theory alone never gave me the feeling of sufficient information for comprehensive understanding. So I started to gain internships and work experience in various fields during the semester breaks, participating in panel discussions and visiting fringe groups. For example, I was a lobbyist in Brussels for the state of Baden-Württemberg, a survey officer for a census or an editorial assistant in the stock exchange studio of state television. European politics quickly became my favourite. With the Young European Federalists, I learned how non-party political work works with statutes, meetings and information events. As soon as this youth organisation started to become party political, I resigned.

The political left was represented at the university campus because there was a branch of the German Federation of Trade Unions that had offered the antifascist movement premises. I talked to these persons and learned about their fascination with Karl Marx and open borders worldwide. They told me about their fear of the exploitation of many humans and nature for the benefit of a few rich capitalists. When I asked them about their concept of open borders, no one could answer me. When I read Karl Marx, i.e. Capital and the Manifesto of the Communist Party, I had to read a lot of hate and agitation, but hardly found any solutions as to what exactly the new system should look like. When I took part in the student protests against tuition fees, I experienced left-wing activists. It was hardly possible to formulate demands or proposals because any kind of leadership of the assembly was rejected as too authoritarian and there was no negotiation at all with supposedly system-loyal staff of the university's presidium, only blockades. The blockade of the highway and the main railway station prevented tuition fees, but the negotiation of less co-determination of students in shaping their studies through the Bologna Reform and their college as a foundation university was not possible. As a result of these experiences, I developed my ideas on the communitarisation of states and continents towards the united states of the world.

I sought out the political right at a demonstration in Frankfurt. I asked people why they were there. I asked a bald guy in a bomber jacket first, but he just said, "Fuck off, you tick!" Others were more forthcoming. One woman told me about her fear of being wiped out as a human with light skin, blue eyes and blond hair because dark eyes, skin and hair are dominant genetic traits. A man told me about his fear of losing German culture and virtues such as punctuality or thoroughness due to mass immigration of humans with a different religion, language, script, family structure, idea of leisure time and way of educating their children. The woman's and man's approach to the problem was to limit immigration and, as in the past, to protect the borders. In times of the uncertainties of globalisation, they longed to go back to the last known time when they thought the world was still in order. As a result of this encounter, I developed my ideas on cultural protection areas.

I looked for religious extremists in mosques and finally found them during a Quran distribution campaign in the Offenbach pedestrian zone. At a previous action in Frankfurt,

I had already obtained a Koran and started reading it. I had made notes with contradictions, which I pointed out to the professing Salafist. For example, why God is called the All-merciful but does not show mercy to unbelievers. The Salafist looked up a PDF document on his mobile phone. I asked him what he was doing and he said he was looking up the passage in a Koran exegesis. When I said that I couldn't accept that because these writings don't come from God, but from a human, he agreed with me. His solution was to turn Germany into a Muslim state of God. I could understand that he believed in something different than I did, and that faith is something fundamentally different than knowledge. As a result of this encounter, I developed my ideas on religious communities and religious management.

5.5.5 Training

After graduation, I filmed the committee process in the form of a TV show with the help of students I had met in the course of my studies in the drama seminar and UniTV. The attempt to market this show format failed due to rejections from broadcasters and production companies. After that I started working as an educator and did the training. I can deal well with children because they often simply tell the truth and give free rein to their feelings. I got to know the psyche of a human better and was able to gain leadership experience. Reading people like a book, recognising their wishes and fears, being able to win them over for my purposes without coercion was the goal of these insights.

As I had decided at the age of 18, I started to make this book out of the idea diary after graduation. As a Diploma in Political Science with various practical work experiences, I felt qualified enough. During my studies I wanted to learn who is to blame for bad policies, wanted to understand how the system works and who is responsible for it. I started writing this book while I was training to be an educator and realised that faults in the system are responsible for the ills. The faults in the system were committed by humans when they had to hastily invent a new system after a revolution. All the humans thereafter adapted to these faults as best they could without questioning them.

5.6 My first experience with politics

In my youth, I grew up in a suburb of a city with a high proportion of foreigners from the Middle East and North Africa. I was afraid of violent foreigners and thought it was in their genes to be like that. Then, at the age of 17, I questioned my hatred of foreigners and wanted to know why young foreigners are prone to violence. I made friends with notorious foreigners and then asked them directly about it. They told of losing their parents' social status, prestige and home after immigration. Life with many siblings in a small space, a frustrated father who sits at home partly unemployed, giving orders and beating, and a mother who obeys her husband. This created the need to get out of the flat and into the streets, to numb themselves with drugs, to earn money from drug dealing in order to buy status symbols and drugs, and to accost or beat passers-by in order to feel powerful towards them. The feeling of powerlessness to achieve the status, education and income of the domestic generated envy. This was to be balanced by the feeling of physical superiority and power over fearful and small-mouthed locals. When I learned this, I wanted to know how and why the parents came to Germany. While studying political science, I took the necessary seminars and learned everything I needed to know. In the 1960s, full employment was achieved because so many domestic men had died in the war. But the occupiers wanted to get compensation payments and profits out of their occupation zones. Thus began the guest worker policy, which never deserved its name. As is well known, guests leave, but guest workers settled with their families and stayed. This deception of the domestic population and the deception of the immigrants sowed early seeds of ill will between domestic citizens and foreigners. The colour of skin, hair and eyes made it obvious which part of the population a resident belonged to. Germans were still influenced by the racist policies of the pre-war period and were forced by occupiers to accept the conditions as losers. The basic conditions were conceivably bad for a successful integration of immigrants that could ensure peaceful coexistence. Initially, immigration policy was limited to Europe, but by the 1970s it had spread to the Middle East and North Africa. The Italians and Ottomans were allied with Germany in the war and provided a large proportion of the guest workers for a long time. Over time, after the colonies were dissolved, states were created and borders drawn without including the populations there. This created a power vacuum in exploited countries with a battered and ignored population. In a power vacuum, the law of the strongest applies because the state is not in a position to establish a functioning monopoly on the use of force. The states had to get into debt from the industrialised nations that had once exploited them and have since been caught in the spiral of powerlessness, fear and poverty. Weapons supplies from the forges of the industrial nations provide the necessary means of oppression for tyrannies. Food supplies or tax-subsidised food at dumping prices prevent the development of sufficient agriculture in developing countries. Corporations from industrialised nations have branches in underdeveloped countries and thus deprive this country of the profits from their business. They tax the profits in industrialised nations and distribute them to pensioners there as part of their private pensions or to investors living in tax havens or on yachts.

This made it clear that the fundamental fault lies in the political system and not in the genes of the humans. That made me hopeful, because rules made by humans can be changed, laws of nature cannot.

5.7 My image of humans

Basically, I believe in the good in humans. Humans only become evil when they have experienced more suffering than joy in their lives. My image of humans is shaped by biology and psychology. Every human being belongs to the same species. All humans can produce fertile offspring together. Therefore, all humans have the same conditions and should be treated equally. By nature, humans are herd animals and seek social interaction with their fellow species. Humans are unequal in their temperaments, talents and races. Only after birth do they adapt to their environment, develop virtues and cultures and learn to imitate the role models of their society. The strength of humans is their adaptable brain. Compared to animal species, humans cannot survive on their own after birth. They learn to survive in their age and can use all the technical achievements of their ancestors in a very short time. The long period of growing up to the age of majority is unique in the animal kingdom. Affection and love therefore play a special role when humans look for partners to beget and raise children. The more hatred and violence are involved, the more likely children are to adapt to a behaviour of hatred and violence. This is how humans pass on behaviour to each other. Since records and data have been kept, more and more behaviours are being passed on from generation to generation. In the past, religion was the filter for good and bad behaviour, today it is state policy.

Humans may have caused a lot of harm in the past, but they can change the future today in a self-determined way. Democratically and digitally run states let their inhabitants decide on good and bad behaviour. Behaviour that is considered good by the majority is accepted and that which is considered bad is rejected. However, there are certain humans who have special characteristics, behaviours, opinions or attitudes that are rejected by the rest of the humans. In the vernacular, these special humans are called black sheep. *I do not want to whitewash black sheep, but to give them a niche to survive in, where they can flock.* Municipal self-government and cultural protection areas make this possible. Borders are necessary so that humans can come together in groups and live together in niches on earth. Living together is characterised by solidarity and peace when humans come together voluntarily and form their own culture of living together. Democratic co-determination makes this possible.

If some humans are forced to live together out of necessity, envy, resentment and criminality arise. As long as every human being can look for his or her own like-minded people, the responsibility lies with him or her. *Humans grow with their responsibility.* If he does not receive responsibility and is regulated by others, he reacts with resentment or rebellion. If he is given responsibility, he can prove himself, gain self-confidence, fail and learn from his faults. As long as a political system offers humans more advantages for deeds that benefit or do not damage the general public, they will adapt to it.

5.8 My first concept from 2009

In 2009, I applied for a TV show called "I can chancellor". For the audition video, I wrote a text that I recited in the video. The places in brackets are the filming locations. In the audition form I had to answer questions. All the content can be found in detail in this book today. The language, on the other hand, is more like what I thought at the age of 25.

5.8.1 Introduction video

Dear reigns, I can be chancellor because I have studied economics as well as politics and because I know how important your fiscal contribution is for my budget. I offer you an excellent infrastructure for the movement of persons and goods, less bureaucracy in setting up and running a company, but a company auditing agency that issues risk badges, a simple tax system with 20% business tax and no wage tax. (Frankfurt, Central Station, Stock Exchange)
Dear people, I can be chancellor because I have sought training as a chancellor. I know where the shoe pinches, because I grew up with them. So how about: social welfare in which everyone gets what they need to stand on their own two feet again. Full employment through innovative quality products produced by them. Open nursery schools around the clock so that they can combine their family with any appeal. A social emergency hotline that helps before it is too late. (Allotment gardens, park bench, suburban railway, petrol station at night, Offenbach).
Hello children, I can be a chancellor because I studied social psychology as well as politics and I know how stupid adults can be sometimes. I offer you: an environment where you can run around and play. A school where you have more say in what you

want to learn. Youth centres that you have to build and care for yourselves. Leisure facilities that are fun even without a TV or games console. (Playground, Mühlheim)

Dear politicians, I can be chancellor because I am happy to work with them. No party line can stop me from achieving new goals with them. I see them as colleagues and confederates who share the same hobby as I do. I offer them: constant campaigning, a reliable coalition partner who is ready to put good ideas into practice with any party, cheeky sayings, heated debates, but in any case a lot of fun at work with the necessary dash of self-irony. (First German Parliament, Frankfurt)

Ladies and gentlemen, you have now gained an insight into how I would make policy with you. For this to work, I need them! I need your opinion and I need your vote! So please, vote for me and we will do democracy. (Quarries, Mühlheim)

5.8.2 Interview form

Hobbies: politics, psychology, economics, research, technology, media, news, friends, partying, sex, music

Interests: Learning, teaching, inventing, debating, finding compromises, filming knowledge, laughing, making faces, whistling, dancing

Party membership: No, I am not in a party. Instead, I am in a political organisation. In the Young European Federalists (JEF), the youth organisation of the European Union, I am the deputy leader of the Hesse regional association.

Which political party are you closest to?: None! There are good approaches in every party. I am open to everything that helps the humans inland to live better. I give weight according to my subjective feelings, which are shaped by my environment and my studies.

What goals and positions are important to them?: My political position is neither right, nor left, nor centre. It is synthetic! My goal is to create the best out of everything through dialogue. All remits or areas of life are relevant for the harmony of humans and nature.

Fascination with the office of Federal Chancellor: The possibility of being taken seriously by influential personalities *fascinates me as much about the office of Federal Chancellor as implementing my ideas and leaving my children a country worth living in and loving.*

Why does Germany need you as Chancellor: *Because I know and appreciate humans from all walks of life, I'm not a party soldier, I'm kind to others and honest, and because Germany must have experienced my reforms in 2030 so that history doesn't repeat itself.*

Election slogan: *WE make democracy*

Ideas for Germany: *My ideas for Germany now fill an A4 file folder. I've wanted to become chancellor since my college entrance qualification and have been collecting them all, day by day. After my Diploma, I will turn them into a novel, which will also be made into a film. My ideas are interwoven in an overall concept. The fragments only unfold their full effect in composition. The exact course of the book will probably not take reality, because not everyone thinks the way I do. But that doesn't matter. The main thing is that everyone knows what it's about and gets involved.*

5.9 My procedure

Here I describe how I went about writing this book. Based on my experiences, I developed ideas, wrote them down on pieces of paper and notepads and put them together in the idea diary. Then followed several run-throughs to completion. I wrote down all the work steps for each run-through in an auxiliary document like a logbook. This gave me a work instruction that I could use to work on all the volumes in a uniform way. In the first run-through, I typed up all the notes from the idea diary, left out nonsense, photographed all the drawings, sorted all the ideas and divided them into ministries. I saved technical ideas that are legally protectable in a separate document.

In the second run-through, I sorted all the ideas within a ministry, eliminating the unnecessary and the duplicated. From each idea I made a feasible proposal. With some friends I went through individual ministries and asked for feedback. Based on all the ideas, I wrote a constitution, using the constitutions of Switzerland and the Canton of Bern as an aid. I went through all the organigrams of all the federal ministries and Bavarian state ministries. I included what fit and what was missing, left out what was unnecessary and combined what was duplicated. Then I sorted all the constitutional articles and all the departments and units from the organisation charts into the appropriate ministries in the book.

In the third run-through, I sorted the tables of contents of all ministries, mentioned matching constitutional articles in the matching chapter and linked them with a footnote. I inserted the keywords from the organigrams into the chapters. Articles, departments and chapters were aligned with each other, thus revising the constitution continuously. At the end, I wrote the objectives, departments and tasks of each ministry.

In the fourth run-through, I adapted everything to each other and found uniform wording. All tables of contents were sorted uniformly. Duplications were deleted and texts longer than one page were shortened and divided into sub-chapters. The constitution was reordered and all articles renumbered.

In the fifth run-through, the conversion of the old ministries was inserted so that it is clear which departments and units of which federal and state ministries are included in the respective new ministry. The summary of all ministries and the derivation was written. Corrections by proofreaders have been inserted. For the international version, terms referring to Germany were replaced by neutral phrases.

6 Notes to the reader

Dear reader, thank you for reading this book. I hope it will make you and your fellow human beings happy. Please always remember that I am only human. I cannot know everything and I make faults. Because the book is extensive, I am giving you an instruction manual and appropriate hints. I hope this will help you find your way between the volumes. When you understand what I am trying to do, you can find the right adjustments for you. I hope that you will then be able to use as much as possible yourself and not need me. If you do, I hope to be able to give you advice and support.

6.1 Operating instructions

This book consists of 21 volumes. The first volume is the summary. It provides an overview of all the remaining volumes in less than 10% of the total number of pages. To make it easy for you to find your way around, all the headings are named the same as the titles of the individual volumes. In the sections under the headings you will find words in bold. They are called the same as individual chapters in the volume that is being summarised.

The second volume is the derivation. It picks you up in the current times with their political problems and social challenges. So that you can put yourself in my position, you will also learn something about me and my attitudes towards humans, nature and politics. So that you can become active yourself to help yourself and others, you will also get tips there.

The third volume is the constitution. It is written as constitutions are usually written and consists of numbered chapters, articles and paragraphs. It describes all the basic rights of residents, domestic nationals, state employees and politicians. It provides the stage on which the new political system will take place. Therefore, the exact procedure is not described there, only the principles. The headings of the individual articles contain footnotes that tell you in which volumes the respective articles can be found.

The remaining 18 volumes are the ministries. In these, all policy areas are covered and sorted into the appropriate responsibilities of ministries. All these volumes have a similar structure. At the beginning, you will find out which objectives are pursued, which departments are responsible and which tasks are carried out. In the middle, you find out what policies are implemented in that ministry and which offices are responsible for them. Whenever other ministries are responsible for something, there is a footnote. It tells you in which volume and in which chapter this responsibility is described. Whenever constitutional articles are affected by a chapter, there is a footnote in the relevant heading. It tells you which article and which paragraph is affected. At the end, you will find out how the current situation has to be adapted to the new system so that it can be introduced. Because this new system can be applied in all states and human gatherings worldwide, it was not possible to mention all of them. I have used Germany as an example because I live there and know this system best. You will learn in the last chapter of each of these 18 volumes how the current form of government, policy and the departments of the ministries are maintained, changed or abolished. All the details based on this, which are not mentioned in any volume, are up to the citizens, parties or employees of the ministries. Ultimately, you decide how much of what you learn in my book you want to put into practice.

The last page in each volume is a contact form. There you will find out where and how you can get in touch with me and what possibilities this opens up for you. Firstly, you have the opportunity to send me suggestions for improvement if you don't like individual proposals and have a different suggestion for a solution. Secondly, you can find readers who, like you, want to implement things from this book and build up a network of contacts. For example, you can form a labour union, a Residential Community, a company, an association, a club or a political party together. Thirdly, you can donate money so that the newly founded party or contact network in your country can pay for staff, materials and advertising in order to be able to implement as many of the projects from this book as possible. Fourthly, you can found a party in your country with which you can put the proposals from this book to the election of your people. You will receive a statute and a party programme. All other readers from your country who want to found a party will then be forwarded to you so that they can join the party. As a party member, you can take on tasks and make adjustments.

Tasks range from reading from the book to volunteers, canvassing voters, holding office within the party or a ministry, and standing for election as a member of parliament, council or government.

You can make adjustments by submitting proposals for improvements on how a described goal can be achieved more effectively and in a more generally acceptable way. If there are some proposals that are different from those described in this book, you can found a new party wing. If there are many proposals, you should rather found a new party yourself.

You can also adapt the requirements in this book to the local and personal circumstances in your area. Membership applications are sorted by region and you can contact all party members, especially those who live near you, so that you can form a local group.

6.2 Numbers and numerals

You will often read numbers written as numerals rather than letters in this book. This is because, whenever possible, I have included a margin that you or the voters can determine. For example, I wrote "3 children" and not "three children" because it could have been more or less. In this example, when I talk about carpooling, I have no way of knowing whether there is a car or a bus to transport children. Often it is also down to the harshness of the decision. For example, I can write that there should only be 3% foreigners, but the population is happy with 30%. This procedure is particularly effective when voting is held and those entitled to vote can give numbers themselves. In the final result, the average or median can then simply be calculated from all the numbers cast. In laws, numbers are helpful when only the numbers need to be changed to adapt a law and not the wording. Generally, I wrote all numbers as numerals when I wanted a democratic voting on the number to take place. But if I wanted to set a unique number, you will see the number written out in letters.

6.3 Male form

Except in the constitution, the masculine form is used in all volumes. This is because of my two basic attitudes. Firstly, I think it is good when male authors write in the masculine form and female authors write in the feminine form. I think this opinion could become the law because it doesn't discriminate against anyone, but puts the author or writer first. Readers also find it exciting to know which text or paragraph was written by a woman or a man. Secondly, I told myself at the beginning of the book that I wanted to write this book for all humans. Because "the human" has a masculine article, I kept it that way throughout. If I had chosen "the person", I would have written everything in the feminine form. This is important to mention because women enjoy exactly the same rights as all other genders in the dynamic media democracy. I wrote the constitution, but in the end it is written by a people together, and there are always men and women represented.

6.4 Unpopular proposals

You will certainly find proposals in this book that you don't like. I have tried to do justice to every human being, but I am not perfect. Please do not let this distract you from the overall impression. Feel encouraged to develop counter-proposals and use them to found a new party wing. In the new policy system, you will then have the opportunity to rally supporters behind your counter-proposal and convince the majority in a voting. According to the dynamic media democracy, the people can decide which of my proposals should apply, which should be changed and which proposal should be rejected. If, however, you are in the minority with your Counter-proposal, please consider whether it would be possible to rally enough like-minded people around you. Then you could show your way of life in your municipality or in a cultural protection area. In the new system, you will then have a place reserved for you, where you can continue your way of life without damaging others.

6.5 Suggestions for improvement

If your imagination develops ideas while reading, please write them down. If you can use them to develop suggestions for improvement, I would be happy to hear them. If you like, you can send them to me. You will find the address in the contact form on the last page. If you prefer to send them to another party, I would be happy as well. If you would like to make your own suggestions for improvement, you can do so at any time as a party member of the dynamic People's Party. To do this, you submit a motions and if not all party members agree, you form a party wing. Please always add to your proposal which ministry is responsible for it. You can choose between Labour, Foreign Affairs, Education, Family, Finance, Health, Infrastructure, Innovation, Integration, Digital, Justice, Media, Security, State Organisation, Barter Economy, Planned Economy, Social Market Economy or Free Market Economy. If several ministries are affected, you can also indicate several of these remits.

6.6 Inventions

When I kept my idea diary, I also came up with many ideas that can be realised as a company or product. For many of these ideas, an industrial property right can be applied for, for example a patent. That can happen to you too. Please also write down these ideas or make drawings of them. First and foremost, they belong to you and you can do what you want with them. In the new system, you have the opportunity to become a co-owner of a People's Innovation Company as an inventor. A large part of the profits from your idea then replaces tax money and a small part goes to you. I would like to donate a large part of my So-called technical ideas to the peoples who have voted with an absolute majority in an election for the introduction of dynamic media democracy.

6.7 Become active

In this book you will find a clear goal, namely to ensure the survival of humanity without damaging humans and nature. If you agree with this goal, feel motivated to realise it in the course of your lifetime. Many paths can lead you to this goal. Pay attention to your fellow human beings and follow them if you like their way. If you don't like their way, invent your own way and try to convince as many humans as possible to follow it with you. I have given you many ways to get involved. Or maybe you have developed your own ideas about how you want to get involved. No matter how you want to do it, please do it.

6.8 Game of Life

In the game of life I want to show you how I imagined life and a life course. It was a help for me to go through life. Don't feel compelled to do the same, but take with you what seems useful and friendly. Because all the formulations are taken almost verbatim from the idea diary, the writing is in italics.

6.8.1 Welcome to the game of life

You are a game piece, your name is human, your playing field is called Earth. Like all your fellow players, you have a mind. It is located between your ears. It is the same for all players, only the experiences are different. After your birth, your mind is in the learning phase. Its power grows by 100 million connections per minute in the first year. With the help of this power, you can get to know the world into which you were born. What you learn now will shape you for the rest of your life. If you experience more good than bad, you will believe that the world is good and vice versa. After 10 to 15 years, your mind grows again as much as it did after you were born. Now comes the talent phase. You learn to use the new power in your mind. At first it confuses you, but later you know where your strengths and weaknesses lie. You are now ready to play for your life with your teammates. Humans like to distinguish between children and adults, but it doesn't matter. The power of your mind grows only twice in your life. After 20 to 30 years, the power of your mind degrades every day. How fast that goes and what you have left at the end of your life depends on how you have used your mind over the years.

6.8.2 Welcome to the 21st century

Today, the rules of the game are no longer determined by muscle power alone. It is also the power of money, knowledge and contacts. These forces are invisible and yet they can beat you.

What matters is how you use your mind to access and deal with these forces. It varies in countries and cultures, but if you recognise regularities, you can use them. Our motorised digital age gives you the opportunity to get money, knowledge and contacts regardless of time and space.

You can get money if you manage to avoid the people who earn money with money. So try to be a landlord or employer yourself. If you were poor when you started, you will have to be a tenant and employee for a while. But if you use your mind to get enough knowledge and contacts, you can make it. Money has the advantage that you can store it. As long as you don't gamble with it, you can secure your future with it.

You get knowledge in schools, colleges, seminars, clubs and internships. Wherever humans share their knowledge with other humans, you can be there and learn from them. Be nice to them and you get more. Be diligent and you retain more. Learning knowledge is like sport for your mind. But be careful, because knowledge is fleeting. It fades away if you don't use it. But if you use it and learn more, you can stack it and connect it so that it stays with you.

You get contacts if you are nice and useful. Your mind helps you to assess your fellow human beings. What might they need? What might they like? Some humans should get in touch with you, but don't really want to? Convince them otherwise. Make them happy and they will remember you fondly. Ask them politely for a favour and they will help you.

6.8.3 Welcome to the system

You are never alone in the world. You are always playing in a system that gives you rules. If you violate these rules, the system prevents you from achieving your goals. Be careful and proactive if you want to change the system or if the system changes. If humans are unhappy with the system, they tell the powerful. The powerful are humans with a lot of control over money, knowledge and contacts. If the powerful do not fulfil the wishes of the dissatisfied, there are three possibilities. First, the discontented can become discouraged and resign themselves to their fate. Second, malcontents may resort to violence and terror. Or thirdly, malcontents can organise money, knowledge and contacts and compete with the powerful by beating them at their own game. If you want to join the struggle of the disaffected to change the rules of the game through the third option, then do the following: First see if there are other systems in other places with rules of the game that you like better and go there. Stay away from malcontents who use violence, because the powerful have power to use more violence. Do not start a game that you cannot win. Use your mind to know when it is better for you to admit defeat. Do not show false pride. To admit defeat is not a disgrace, but a sign of a wise mind that knows when to yield in order to make a turn on the way through the game of life.

6.8.4 Welcome to the finish

What is all this for? For the goal of your life. All humans play with each other for their lives. But every human has his own mind. Your mind will tell you what is the goal of your life. When? When you have gained enough experience through trial and mistake to be able to distinguish between cause and effect. Then you will realise what makes you happy and what you have to do for it. Some goals you can achieve by yourself, others you can only achieve together with other humans. No matter how you find the rules of the game, if you want to achieve the goal of your life, then use your mind to live with these rules, to use them to your advantage and to make yourself happy without causing damage to others.

Contact form

Dear reader
If you would like to make what you have read come true, in whole or in part, together with other like-minded people, I offer you several possibilities with this contact form. Fill it out, tear out the page and send it by post to:
Andreas Seidl, P.O. Box 1206, 63488 Seligenstadt / Germany

Or send the details to:
Phone: 0049 1522 818 2243 (whatsapp, telegram, signal)
Email: andreas.seidl2022@web.de

Please mark with a cross:
O   I want to found a dynamic People's Party.
O   I want to donate money for implementation.
O   I want contacts with like-minded people in my area.

Forename: _____

Surname: _____

Please fill in only the contact option through which a reply should be made.

Street, house no.:   _____

Postcode, city, country: _____

Phone: _____

Email address: _____